THE MOUNT JEFFERSON
WILDERNESS GUIDEBOOK

Spire Rock from the Triangulation Trail

THE MOUNT JEFFERSON WILDERNESS GUIDEBOOK
Including the Big Meadows and Triangulation Peak Recreation Areas

by Tony George

The Solo Press • Salem • Oregon

All photos are by the author unless otherwise credited. Illustrations by Vivienne Torgeson

Library of Congress Catalog Card Number: 83- 61705

ISBN 0-913353-00-0

Published by:

The Solo Press
1665 A Street NE
Salem, Oregon 97301

ACKNOWLEDGEMENTS

Unless you have the help and assistance of a great many people, you cannot achieve your dreams. The preparation of this book was no exception. With the greatest appreciation, I would like to acknowledge the contribution of the following individuals to the research and writing of this book.

From the Forest Service, Warren Seaward, Ed Dyer, Melissa Carlson, Ray Crist and Dave Black were most generous in providing information and advice.

Vivienne Torgeson ably produced the maps and graphics. Jim Norman printed all my negatives. Bill Jasper and Bob Anderson assisted in the review and editing of the draft text. Bob Rogers assisted with his publishing advice and support. Owen Daly provided final text editing.

Larry Cox was the person who first introduced me to Oregon's wilderness areas by talking me into climbing the South Sister.

Senator Hatfield graciously agreed to write the foreword, for which I am most grateful.

But the greatest note of appreciation must go to my wife Connie. I could not have attempted this book without her love and support.

Thank you all.

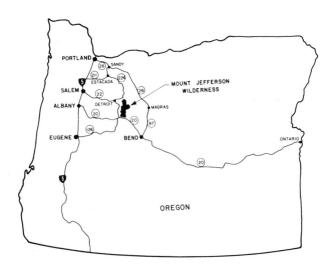

PREFACE

The Mount Jefferson Wilderness is a very popular place to hike and camp. My goal in writing this guidebook is not to encourage more people to use the area, but to prevent overuse and abuse. With the knowledge that regardless of what I write, more people will use this wilderness area in the future, I have tried to write a book which will help you avoid heavily used areas and find areas where you will have more solitude.

First, I have tried to point out the most crowded areas where you are apt to find lots of people. These are the areas most often covered in popular hiking guides, newspapers and magazines, whose stories are designed to increase sales rather than serve the wilderness. Jefferson Park and Marion Lake are examples of beautiful areas which have been heavily promoted, and which are now suffering from overuse and crowding.

Second, I have attempted to provide all the information you will need to seek out a quality recreational experience amidst solitude and seclusion. Is there a lake where you can take your family? Is it stocked with fish? Are there places to camp? You should find answers to these questions, and more, in this guide.

The preparation of this guidebook has only served to increase my interest in the Mount Jefferson Wilderness. After hiking all the trails and visiting most of the lakes, I continue to be tempted by the many ideas for future trips tucked away in the maps and tables. I have years of exploration and adventure to share with my companions. I hope you will too.

Three Fingered Jack from Marion Lake

FOREWORD

As one who grew up and spent a good portion of my adult life in the Salem area, I have a great appreciation for the Mt. Jefferson area and its related features, especially Marion Lake. But in addition to these more conventional reasons for my enthusiasm for Tony George's book is the fact that the Mt. Jefferson Wilderness was my first involvement as a federal legislator in wilderness designation; it was my first "wilderness experience" as a member of the United States Senate.

Since that time, I have been involved in numerous wilderness controversies, seeking the proper but elusive balance between wilderness preservation and development of our National Forests in Oregon. That has been no easy task, but one of its rewards is looking back at the wilderness system we have built in our state. Certainly there can be little argument about having protected the Mt. Jefferson area.

This is partly so because the Mount Jefferson Wilderness offers such a range of experiences. It has magnificent vistas and scenery, trails for backpackers and hikers, and Marion Lake with its long history of family recreational use.

While these are important attributes, the unique feature which wilderness should provide is the opportunity for solitude. Contemporary American society has become extremely urban and complex, with serious impacts upon interpersonal relationships. Dealing with stress has become a major concern in American communities.

For many, wilderness can provide the space necessary for contemplation and reflection. With man simply as a visitor, wilderness allows us the humbling experience of being just a part, rather than the dominating force, of this environment.

With its emphasis on avoiding those areas within the Mount Jefferson Wilderness which already receive heavy use, this book should be an aid to those who seek that solitude. I was proud to sponsor the legislation to designate this wonderful area as wilderness, and am pleased that this guide will assist those who wish to enjoy it.

Senator Mark O. Hatfield

CONTENTS

PART 1:
Introduction

THE WILDERNESS AND RECREATION AREAS

The Mount Jefferson Wilderness, created by an act of nature over millions of years, was preserved as it is today by an Act of Congress in 1968. Unlike other parts of the National Forest, the wilderness is an area where man is a visitor who does not remain. Permanent developments, motorized travel and habitation are restricted so that the area will retain its primeval character. Once preserved, the wilderness becomes an area where you can hike, climb, fish or hunt in a natural setting, without the sights and sounds of the mechanized world.

At slightly over 100,000 acres, the Mount Jefferson Wilderness is the fifth largest wilderness in Oregon. Elevations range from the 10,497-foot-high summit of Mount Jefferson down to 3200 feet on the mountain's west and east sides. The greatest part of the area lies between 4000 and 6000 feet, with the snow-free season at the lower elevations running from June to mid-October.

Its proximity to major population centers, together with its many lakes, miles of trails, and outstanding landscapes, makes this the second most popular wilderness in Oregon. Only the Three Sisters Wilderness, which is more than twice as large, has slightly more recreational use per year. Fifty percent of all use is concentrated in three areas— Marion Lake, Pamelia Lake, and Jefferson Park. The remainder of the area, with over 150 lakes and 200 miles of trails, receives scant use. Obviously, there are still adequate opportunities for solitude if you know where to look.

Introduction

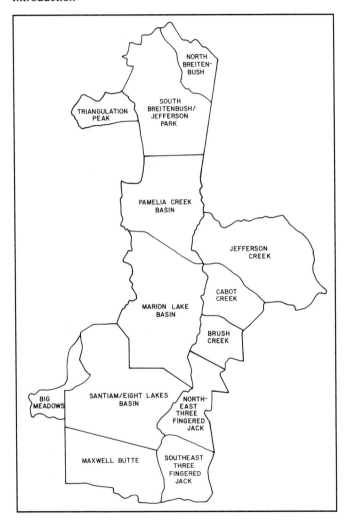

FIGURE 1: MOUNT JEFFERSON WILDERNESS AREA MAP

The Big Meadows and Triangulation Peak Recreation Areas are contiguous to the Mount Jefferson Wilderness and have been used by hikers and other recreationists much as if they were wilderness (see Figure 1). The Big Meadows area contains several lakes which are stocked with fish, and both areas have many miles of trails—some of which serve as alternative access trails into the Mount Jefferson Wilderness.

Although the Big Meadows and Triangulation Peak areas are roadless, they were not included in the Mount Jefferson Wilderness when it was created by Congress. In response to the recreation potential of the two areas, the Forest Service has designated them as Non-motorized Dispersed Recreation Areas. While this allows some logging to occur, the primary emphasis for future management is to promote recreation use. Recreation management plans for the development of trails, campsites, and interpretive displays are being prepared and will be implemented in the future.

Wildlife is abundant in the wilderness and the recreation areas. Deer, elk, bear, coyote, beaver, and marten are but a few of the mammals which call the wilderness home. Many species of birds can be seen in the area, both as residents and during their annual migrations. Fish are stocked by air in many of the lakes. Several lakes have self-sustaining populations, requiring no stocking.

Today, aged Douglas fir and ponderosa pine stand watch over these areas as they have for hundreds of years. Hillsides are covered with huckleberries and scrub trees, testament to earlier forests, burned by wild fire, which today are still in the process of recovery. It has always been this way in the wilderness, the natural processes leading the visitor on a path of discovery into the past and the future. Glaciers advance and recede, gouging valleys and cutting ridges across the landscape. Avalanches thunder down slopes in the winter, leaving piles of debris and naked slopes—new homes for the avalanche lily. The Indians no longer walk the trails first traveled by the ancestors of modern deer and elk, but the trails are there, waiting to be explored.

As you use the area described in this guidebook, you will become conscious of its moods, its history and its future. It is a living, changing and sometimes fragile ecosystem, that will wither under the weight of a single boot, but which will also strike out with hostility toward the unmindful and ill prepared. We are fortunate indeed to have such a resource so short a distance from the major population centers of the northwest.

HOW TO USE THIS GUIDEBOOK

This guidebook provides the most complete and comprehensive information yet prepared for the Mount Jefferson Wilderness. It does not try to hold your hand and walk you down the trail. If you can find the trailhead, you can certainly follow the trail. Rather, all the information you will need to plan a trip in the wilderness is provided in tabular and narrative format. It is up to you to select where you want to go and how you want to get there. Hopefully, the format will allow you to plan more interesting trips to places you have never been.

There is little attempt to judge which areas of the wilderness are best. Beauty is in the eye of the beholder, and whether or not a destination is right for you depends on whether you are hiking, camping, fishing, or simply trying to avoid people. Even after you have hiked all the trails and visited all the lakes, only you will be able to describe what is best for you.

Organization

The first three parts of the guidebook provide general information applicable to the entire wilderness. Part 4 provides more detailed information on specific trails and destination areas. For ease of discussion, the Mount Jefferson Wilderness is divided into small areas (see Figure 1). For each area, information is provided on trails, lakes, camping sites, and the amount of use that is most likely to occur. Trail notes are provided to alert you to confusing trail junctions, map errors, and points of special interest.

Access

Access to the many trails within the Mount Jefferson is provided by a network of State highways and Forest Service roads. Some of the Forest Service roads are paved, but the great majority are gravel. Although most of the gravel roads are in relatively good maintenance, road conditions can change rapidly due to slides, snow or intense storms and flooding.

All of the trailheads described within this book (with the exception of the Two Springs Trail 70 in the Sisters Ranger District of the Deschutes National Forest) can be reached in a conventional two-wheel drive passenger car. As in any off-highway situation, you should carry some emergency supplies and tools to enable you to bypass a wind-blown tree, or a rock slide.

There are 25 different access trails which lead into the wilderness. Table 1 lists each trail and the Forest Service road numbers you will travel to the trailhead, starting with the

TABLE 1: MOUNT JEFFERSON WILDERNESS ACCESS INFORMATION

Entry Point Trail Name	Entry Point Trail #	Road Access Number(s)	Miles from Trailhead to State Hwy.	Relative Annual Use (percent)
Jefferson Lake	66	1292/1290/12/14	17.5	0.8
Cabot Lake	68	1230/12	13.1	4.0
Brush Creek	69	1230-900/1230/12	13.6	0.0
Two Springs	70	1237/1230/12	12.8	0.4
Bear Valley	83	1235/1230/12	11.1	0.2
Summit	65	1234/1230/12	11.3	8.1
Round Lake	73	1210/12	6.6	1.9
Pacific Crest (S)	2000	845	0.3	9.8
Santiam Lodge	3496	840	0.1	0.2
Maxwell Butte	3391	080	0.5	1.4
Duffy Lake	3427	2267	2.7	7.1
Big Meadows	3427	2257	1.1	0
Pika-Fir	3489	2257	3.4	0
Pine Ridge	3443	2261	5.1	1.7
Marion Creek	3436	2255	4.6	25.1
Bingham Ridge	3421	2253	5.6	0.7
Pamelia Creek	3439	2246	3.8	17.7
Woodpecker Ridge	3442	040	5.5	0.6
Whitewater Creek	3429	2243	7.6	10.1
Triangulation Peak	3373	2233-635	9.4	0.0
Craig	3364	4685-330/46	16.7	0.0
South Breitenbush	3375	4685/46	16.8	1.5
Crown	3362	4685-330/46	20.3	0
Roaring Creek	3361	4685/46	20.3	0
Pacific Crest (N)	2000	4220/46	23.7	8.6

road closest to the trailhead, and ending with the Forest Service road connecting to the closest State highway. The distance from the trailhead to the nearest State highway is also provided. The relative annual use is listed, to show how crowded the parking lot may be during peak periods. Figure 2 schematically shows the road access to each trailhead.

To estimate your approximate driving time in hours, divide the distance to the trailhead by 25 mph. Multiply this number by 60, and you will have the approximate driving time in minutes.

Use Patterns

Figure 3 summarizes the patterns of use within the Mount Jefferson Wilderness. The circled entries represent the number of people who enter the wilderness via a specific trailhead, expressed as a percentage of the total number of people who enter the wilderness each year. For example, 25% of all the people entering the Mount Jefferson Wilderness do so via the Marion Lake trailhead. With more than 26,000 people hiking the area each year, this means that over 6,500 people entered at this one trailhead.

Figure 3 also summarizes the amount of recreation use which occurs within each wilderness area. The numbers within each area represent the area's share of the total recreation use in the wilderness, expressed as a percentage. For example, 22 percent of the wilderness use occurs within the South Breitenbush/Jefferson Park area. (Note: Recreation use is measured in visitor-days. That is, one person using the wilderness for one day represents one visitor-day. Six people using the wilderness for one day represent six visitor-days. In a year, 26,000 people will spend 63,000 visitor-days in the wilderness, each person staying an average of 2.5 days. The

Introduction

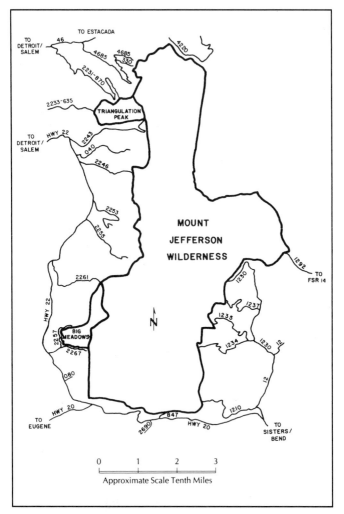

FIGURE 2: MOUNT JEFFERSON WILDERNESS ACCESS MAP

22-percent figure represents slightly less than 14,000 visitor-days, or approximately 5500 people.)

The amount of use which occurs at some of the more popular lakes and destinations is described in the Trail Notes section of the Area Discussions.

A monthly-use bar chart is provided within each Area Discussion. It shows the yearly pattern of use within an area. July is the most popular month in the lower-elevation areas (below 4500 feet), while August is the most popular and crowded month in the higher-elevation areas. Typically, there is very little use after the Labor Day weekend.

A daily-use bar chart is also provided within each Area Discussion. It shows the weekly patterns of use within an area. The weekends will have more than twice as much use as will the weekdays. Wednesday is usually the least crowded day of the week in any area.

Trail Tables

A trail table provides information on all the trails within an area. This includes the trail number, name, length, the total elevation gain and loss, and trail steepness (grade). (If you are interested in looking up a specific trail, but do not know what area it is in, try looking it up in the Trail Index at the end of the guidebook.) Additional information on unusual or unsafe trail conditions will be described in the Trail Notes section for each area.

The trail tables describe the average trail grade in percent. This number is the best indicator of overall trail difficulty. It describes the average trail rise and fall in feet per hundred feet of horizontal travel. If you have to climb up 15 feet and descend 10 feet within 100 feet of trail, then the grade will be $25/100 = .25$, or 25%. The higher the grade number, the

Introduction

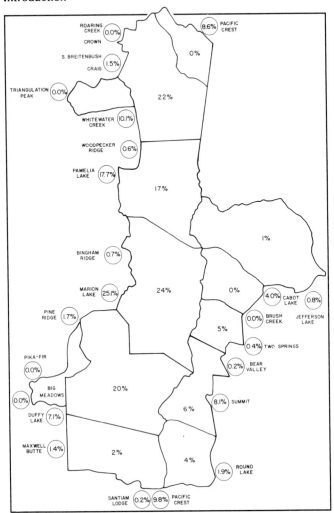

FIGURE 3: USE PATTERN STATISTICS

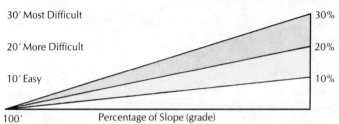

**FIGURE 4: SCHEMATIC OF TRAIL GRADE STEEPNESS—
PERCENT**

steeper will be the average grade of the trail (see Figure 4).

A grade of 0-5% is quite level and is relatively easy to hike—traveling at a pace of 2 miles per hour is often possible, even by unconditioned hikers. A grade of 5-10% is steeper, but it is not difficult to maintain a steady pace of 2 miles per hour if you are in good condition. A grade of 10-15% is steeper yet, and usually requires that a slower pace be set. Sometimes a pace as slow as 1-1.5 miles per hour is typical. A grade of 15-20% is the steepest you will probably encounter over a long distance. Usually, it cannot be hiked comfortably with full pack at a pace faster than 1 mile per hour. Rest breaks will be quite welcome.

The maximum grade listed for each trail is the steepest sustained pitch over several hundred feet of trail. Short sections of trail (less than 100 feet) may be even steeper. As can be seen in the trail tables, trails with modest average grades can have some steep pitches in the shorter stretches.

Just because a trail is steep is no reason to avoid it. Sometimes the steeper trails actually will get you to your destination faster than an easy trail, since they are usually shorter and more direct. Also, many of the steeper trails are to viewpoints—heavy backpacks can be stashed in the bushes along the trail and the trail can be hiked in a short time with relative ease.

Lake Tables

A lake table provides information on all named lakes within an area, even though some lake names are not shown on published wilderness maps or on the campsite maps included in this guidebook. Information provided includes the cross-country distance from the lake to the nearest trail, the distance from the lake to the nearest trailhead, and the number of the trail you should take to get to the lake. The lake's elevation, size and depth are also provided. If the lake is stocked with fish, the type of fish found in the lake is indicated. Finally, the number of existing campsites at each lake is provided.

If you do not know which area a lake is in, you can look it up in the Lake Index in the back of the guidebook.

Campsite Maps

Sketch maps are provided for most of the lakes within an area. These maps show the approximate location of existing campsites in relation to the lake and Forest Service trails. For some areas, the maps also show where additional camps could be made in the event that all available camp sites are used when you arrive. You can use these maps to decide where you might camp in the wilderness.

If you are a fisherman, the water outlines show the approximate location of deeper water. Where appropriate, specific regulations governing use will be noted on the map.

Seasons of Use

In the spring and summer, the snows recede at a somewhat predictable pace. Table 2 provides information on the snow level at different times of the year. It can serve as a rough guide as to when trailheads, trails and lakes of the wilderness will be free of snow. The date when the snow will be completely melted could be earlier or later, depending on the depth of the snow fall during the previous winter.

TABLE 2: HISTORICAL SNOWMELT TRENDS

Elevation	Date Free of Snow
2500	May 1
3500	May 15
4500	June 15
5500	July 15
6500	August 1

RULES AND REGULATIONS

The Mount Jefferson Wilderness

Due to the ever-increasing use of the Mount Jefferson Wilderness, certain rules and regulations have been developed by the Forest Service. Some of these rules are required because of the very nature of the Wilderness Act which created wilderness areas. For instance, motorized vehicles are restricted. Other rules have been developed in an effort to prevent excessive damage to heavily used areas.

Each trail that leads into the wilderness has a trailhead signboard. On this board, the Forest Service posts copies of the latest rules and regulations and any special restrictions or notices. Attached to the board is a permit box containing self-issuing wilderness permits. Before entering the wilderness, you should fill out a permit, leave the copy of the permit in the box provided and keep your copy with a member of your group.

Introduction

The following activities were prohibited within the Mount Jefferson Wilderness at the time of publication. Check the signboard at the trailhead for any changes to these regulations.

(1) Entering the area between June 15 and November 15 without a permit.

(2) Camping on the West Marion Lake peninsula, Scout Lake peninsula and Bays Lake peninsula.

(3) Camping within 100 feet horizontal distance of the high water mark of Marion, Pamelia, Hank's, and Hunts lakes.

(4) Building, maintaining, attending or using a fire, campfire or stove fire within 100 feet horizontal distance of the high water mark of Marion, Pamelia, Hank's, and Hunt's lake.

(5) Grazing livestock within 200 feet horizontal distance of any lake

(6) Using any motorized equipment.

(7) Leaving a fire without completely extinguishing it.

(8) Cutting or chopping any ground vegetation, brush, or standing trees, including snags.

(9) Failing to pack out all litter and camping equipment.

(10) Discharging firearms within 150 yards of a campsite, or across any trail or body of water.

(11) Shortcutting trail switchbacks on foot or horse or with packstock.

(12) Leaving human waste, litter, food scraps, fish entrails, etc. exposed or placing them near or in any body of water.

(13) Camping for a period longer than 16 days during any 30-calendar-day period.

Forest Service wilderness rangers are authorized to issue tickets to individuals who violate the regulations. While it may be discouraging to some that we must have policemen in the wilderness, I find it comforting to know that some effort is being made to protect the wilderness resource for future generations.

Wildlife and fish resources are managed by the Oregon State Fish and Wildlife Commission. Fishing and hunting licenses are required and the area is patrolled by the Oregon State Police to enforce regulations. Users should consult the applicable regulations before entering the area to hunt or fish. Fishermen should be aware that fishing in the outlet of Marion Lake between Outlet Rock and Marion Falls is totally prohibited.

Federal regulations prohibit the removal of any historic or prehistoric cultural resource evidence, including Native American artifacts such as arrowheads. If you should find such material, carefully note the location and report it to the Forest Service for future study. The significance of an artifact can only be determined through careful study by professionals at the site where it was found. Do not remove it.

Warm Springs Indian Reservation

The Warm Springs Indian Reservation is owned and regulated by the Confederated Tribes of the Warm Springs Reservation. Because reservation lands are immediately adjacent to the Mount Jefferson Wilderness on the north and east sides, I have also included some information on the Indian rules and regulations.

In general, the public has no right of access on the reservation lands, except as specifically allowed by the Warm Springs Indians. At present, some access is allowed for fish-

15

ing in special Visitor Fishing Areas, and a fishing permit is required. Permits and fishing regulations are available from the Warms Springs Reservation. Fishing and hiking within the McQuinn Strip, a narrow strip of land along the west and north boundaries of the reservation, is allowed with a valid State of Oregon fishing license. Enforcement of regulations is performed by the Warm Springs Indians according to their own laws. No camping is allowed anywhere on the reservation or the McQuinn Strip, except at designated campgrounds, such as at Breitenbush Lake. For more specific information, consult the Reservation Fishing Regulations.

ROUTE FINDING

Experienced hikers do not need maps, compasses, or anything but their good sense of direction to get around in the wilderness—or so some people would like to think. Unfortunately, every year, someone dubbed "experienced" is reported separated from his or her group. After a great deal of searching, most lost hikers are found safe and sound, and some are not. Rather than be a statistic or a headline in a newspaper, why not make sure you are prepared the next time you go into the wilderness? There are a great many good books on route finding and navigation. If you have no experience in using map and compass, then it is recommended that you buy a good book and read it (see *References*). Regardless of your route-finding abilities, no one should go into the wilderness area without a map (see the *Maps* section if you do not have a map of the area).

After months of traveling the trails in the area, I have learned that trail signs are not reliable, junctions can be confusing, and the land does not always lie the way it is supposed to. Even if you go on a short day hike, the trail may have changed since the last time you were there, or someone may have removed the sign. Moreover, if for no other reason, you can use the map to enhance your appreciation of the area; to identify a distant peak, or the last creek you crossed.

Now that you have a map, you need a compass. Right? Well, not necessarily. If you do not know how to use a compass, it is not going to be very useful. Use your route-finding book to learn how to use a compass. You need to learn how to determine your location by sighting on distant objects (called "taking bearings"). Once you can find out where you are, you need to learn to follow a compass course across varied terrain and around obstacles. The best type of compass to buy is one which is simple and easy to use—a liquid filled compass helps to damp out vibrations and protects the needle from damage. Carry the compass around your neck or in your pocket so it will always be ready. Carrying a compass in your pack is like not carrying a compass at all.

In addition to a compass, if you can afford one, you should buy an altimeter. Modern altimeters can give your elevation accurate to 30 feet. In contrast, most topographic maps have 80 foot contour intervals. Using an altimeter and a contour map, you can almost always determine your location. If you are on a trail, hiking along a ridge, or along a stream, simply read your indicated elevation from the altimeter. Then, check your map to find where the trail or other feature you are following crosses a contour interval of the same elevation and presto, you have found your location. This system will work in fog, whiteouts, and even in the dark.

Introduction

A good altimeter costs between $135 and $150, but when you consider what it can do for you, it is well worth the cost. While researching this book, I was able to detect map errors and find trails that have not been marked on maps in years, by using an altimeter and a map.

If you doubt that you need a map, a compass or even an altimeter, when entering the wilderness, then you should try to find Cincha Lake. It is only 50 yards off one of the most popular trails in the Mount Jefferson Wilderness. Can't guess where it is? Well, get a map and you will find it just off the Duffy Trail #3427. Now get a compass and go try to find it. (Days later . . . .) Still can't find it? Don't feel bad, at least you are not lost. Now if you can borrow an altimeter, drive to the Duffy trail head. Set your altimeter at 4020 feet and walk up the Duffy Trail for approximately 2 miles, until the altimeter reads 4500 feet. You should be able to look at your contour map and check these elevations. At 4500 feet in elevation, look for a small stream crossing the trail, and follow it south. With some luck, you will find Cincha Lake, and maybe even Little Cincha Lake. If you were able to find Cincha Lake, you should be able to go anywhere you want in the wilderness. Later in this guide, you will learn about many places that can only be reached by going cross country. Practice a little at a time. Try to identify streams that you may cross, and distant ridges you may see. Make your routes more complicated each time you go out in the wilderness. Always note your elevation when you leave a trail or other known location to go cross-country. Then if you become disoriented, you can always return to that elevation and traverse back to the point where you left the trail. When you are confident, try to find Craig Lake, or better yet, some of the lakes in the upper

Whiskey Creek basin. Now you will experience some solitude.

MAPS

To effectively use the information provided in this guide-book, and to properly plan your trips and navigate in the Mount Jefferson Wilderness, you must have a map of the area. It will be particularly handy to have a copy of the Forest Service wilderness map (see discussion below), since many comments in this guidebook are referenced directly to this map. You should always carry a map while hiking.

Wilderness Maps

The best overall map you can use in the wilderness is a topographic map. It not only shows where everything is located, but also gives information on the steepness of the terrain and elevations. The only topographic map currently available for the Mount Jefferson Wilderness is produced by the Forest Service. It covers the entire wilderness area at a scale of 1 inch to the mile, and also includes parts of the Warm Springs Indian Reservation. Elevation contours are displayed in 80-foot intervals. But while this map was revised in 1979, it does not include the most recent information on road and trail access, and some trails and trail junctions are shown in the wrong location. Map errors and omissions are discussed in the individual trail notes latter in this guide.

The map entitled "Mount Jefferson Wilderness," is available for sale at any Deschutes, Mount Hood or Willamette National Forest office (1983 cost $1.00).

Topographic United States Geological Survey Quad-rangle Maps also cover the area, but these are not recom-

Introduction

mended. Trail and road information on these maps is terribly out of date, and use of these maps could cause more confusion than assistance.

A new "Mount Jefferson Recreation Map" is reportedly being published and may be in print soon. This topographic map is colored and shaded to provide an impression of the vertical relief. For further information regarding this map, contact: Geo-Graphics
                519 SW 3rd, Suite 418
                Portland, Oregon 97204

Road and Access Maps

There are two general types of access maps available—Forest Recreation Maps and Ranger District Maps. Each National Forest produces a Recreation Map, which is small in scale (0.5 inches to the mile) and relatively general in detail. It shows all the major roads leading to trail heads, but not the small side roads. Forest Recreation maps are updated only once every several years, so they may be out of date. Copies are available for sale at any Deschutes, Mount Hood, or Willamette National Forest office (1983 cost $1.00).

A larger scale (1 inch to the mile) and much more detailed map is sometimes available from individual Forest Service Ranger Districts. These Ranger District Maps are also called "Fireman's Maps". They are revised annually, and provide the most up-to- date information on new roads, trails, and other developments. When available, they are for sale at the District Ranger office (1983 cost $1.00). A copy of the Detroit Ranger District (Willamette National Forest) map and the Sisters Ranger District (Deschutes National Forest) map will provide all the information you need to reach any of the trails within the Mount Jefferson Wilderness.

PART 2:
Some Words on Wilderness Use

WHY DISPERSE USE?

Thousands of people use the Mount Jefferson Wilderness every week during the summer. Just as soon as someone leaves a campsite during a busy week, someone else comes along and pitches camp. This continued use around popular wilderness campsites tends to accelerate the adverse effects that camping has on the area. Vegetation never has a chance to recover from trampling. New plants and grass cannot grow because seeds cannot take root before they too are crushed. Slowly, the size of the campsite increases, with no opportunity for recovery between uses. Wildlife that depends on the forage and water around lakes and in meadows will be forced to leave the area if campsites are continually occupied. Dispersing your use to other areas and off-season periods will help to alleviate this problem.

CAMPING

Regardless of your reasons for wanting to camp in the wilderness, there should be no trace of your presence when you leave. Because many of the available campsites have already been established over years of use, you will not be able to return them to a natural condition. However, you should leave your campsite at least as clean as you found it. If the group before you has left litter, pick it up and pack it out as your contribution to keeping the wilderness a pleasant place.

When campsites are abused by continual use, particularly by large groups, the Forest Service may prohibit further use for several years. These areas are typically roped off by string fences and small signs which read:

WILDERNESS RESTORATION SITE
Please Do Not Walk Through or Camp In This Area

You should avoid these areas and locate your camp at a different site.

Site Selection

In most instances, you will be able to use the *Campsite Maps* to help find a campsite that has already been used by others. If you arrive at your destination, and all the existing sites are in use, some of the maps also show areas that are suitable for making new camps. Generally, they are flat areas without a lot of underbrush. Also, they are outside of the

A typical string-fence sign marking an area where use is temporarily restricted

100-foot No Camping zones established by the Forest Service. If you carry a collapsible water container, you can set up camp a moderate distance from crowded areas and walk to get your water each day.

Avoid camping in meadows, along streambanks and fragile alpine areas. These areas are easily scarred or trampled.

The Forest Service discourages the creation of new campsites or fire rings at any location which has existing campsites. New campsites are allowed when camping in remote areas reached by cross country travel. However, fire rings are discouraged unless absolutely necessary. When you finally do select a campsite, clear only the smallest area necessary for camping, cooking and socializing. When leaving, try to return the area to as near natural condition as possible.

Trenching

Trenching is a practice which was used years ago to prevent rain water from running under open-tarp type tents. Both destructive and unsightly, today it is simply unnecessary. Modern backpacking tents have waterproof floors and are designed for the wettest of conditions. If you have selected a good campsite, rain water will simply be absorbed into the soil or drain away from the tent. Unfortunately, there are still a few people who dig trenches, and even worse, who do not obliterate the trenches when leaving camp. Fill in any trenches you find. Hopefully, trenching will become a thing of the past.

Camp fires and Stoves

Camp fires should be considered a luxury that is indulged in only when it will not cause damage or disturbance to the area or to others. In many areas, wood is being burned faster

23

Some Words on Wilderness Use

An example of needless and unsightly trenches

Fire rings and litter combine to create an unpleasant campsite   25

A site at Pamelia Lake shows why standing trees should not be cut

than dead wood falls to the ground. But availability of wood is not the only reason why camp fires should be used discriminately. When hundreds of people use the same area year after year, the signs of use tend to accumulate. Ashes build up in fire rings, the rings are built bigger, more ashes accumulate, and the pattern continues until someone builds a new ring nearby. In time, the area will be dotted with fire rings.

With the advent of highly reliable and affordable stoves, campers no longer need to build camp fires. Try to avoid the use of fires unless the area is minimally used, the fire is essential, small, and in an existing fire ring. The burning of garbage is recommended, but only if it is burned completely. Unburnt garbage will attract bears and other animals. If you do build a fire, only use wood that can be gathered and carried by hand. Do not put logs on the fire which are so big that they will not burn completely.

Please do not leave garbage for the Forest Service to pack out

Small gas, kerosene or propane stoves are now considered to be an essential part of wilderness travel. They are lightweight, quick, and efficient for boiling water and cooking camp stews. Modern stoves are extremely dependable, particularly when compared to the chances of finding dry wood. On cold winter, spring and fall hikes, your stove can serve up a hot cup of soup or chocolate, or make the difference between life and death in survival situations. Like an American Express Card, don't leave home without it.

Camp Sanitation

For disposal of human waste, carry a light plastic garden shovel. Select a screened spot (for privacy) at least 100 feet from the nearest trail or water source. Dig a hole 6-8 inches deep, or as deep as possible. Burn the toilet paper when there is no fire hazard. All other camp wastes should be packed out, including sanitary napkins and tampons.

27

Some Words on Wilderness Use

A helpful hint to facilitate camp sanitation: when you arrive at camp, the first thing you should do is locate and dig a latrine hole. Then, if nature calls while you are busy cooking, or when you are tent-bound in inclement weather, you can take care of business in the shortest possible time, and in a sanitary manner.

Garbage, cans and bottles should all be stored in plastic bags and packed out. Do not leave garbage for the Forest Service to pick up unless you want them to start charging camping fees to pay for the service. Waste water and dishwater can be poured in the fire pit or in another hole. Never wash or bathe in streams or lakes, as it transmits communicable diseases and pollutes the water. Rather, carry a collapsible wash basin — washing and rinsing some distance from the water source. Biodegradable soap does not degrade in cold alpine waters, and it pollutes the water for fish. If you don't

An "improved" campsite at Alice Lake

want to drink your waste water, don't ask someone else to do so.

Camp Improvements

The only camp improvements that are compatible with wilderness use are those which you can carry on your back. The cutting of boughs and poles for lean-tos and bedding is a destructive practice made obsolete by emergency shelters and foam pads—lightweight alternatives to carrying a metal axe or hatchet. Plastic shelters should be removed when you leave camp. Barbecue grills are best left in the backyard. When left behind in the wilderness, they become rusty and are seldom reused. The same thing goes for cooking cans. Pack them out.

Other improvements such as camp benches made from logs and rocks, might be alright for temporary use, but they should be disassembled when you leave camp.

Water Use and Giardiasis (Backpacker Diarrhea)

Water is abundant throughout most of the Mount Jefferson Wilderness area, except along some sections of the Pacific Crest Trail, the areas east of the crest of the Cascades, and the Maxwell Butte area. There are some developed springs, which are shown on the maps, but they are not treated. All water should be used with caution.

Giardia Lamblia is a small protozoan which lives in the intestines of animals and humans. It can be transmitted by drinking untreated contaminated water—even clear, cold, running mountain water. After drinking the water, the incubation period of the disease is 6-15 days, and may not show up until after your wilderness trip is over. Common symptoms include nausea, abdominal cramps, flatulence, lethargy, diarrhea, and weight loss. You will be truly miserable.

Giardiasis may persist for weeks if untreated. Other types of diseases can also be transmitted through water contamination. Therefore, it makes sense to treat all water while in the wilderness—either by boiling, chemicals, or water purifiers.

GROUP SIZE

Group size is not regulated within the Mount Jefferson Wilderness. However, large groups are not encouraged. The optimum group size for travelling in the wilderness is 4-6. If an individual is sick or injured, someone can stay with the victim while at least two companions go for help. Also, most campsites cannot accommodate more than two or three tents. When larger groups go into the wilderness, it is best to break up into smaller groups while travelling and camping. Evening socialization should also be done in small groups.

BEARS

Black bears inhabit the forested areas throughout the Mount Jefferson Wilderness. Although secretive in nature, bears are dangerous animals. You should always be alert to potential conflicts with bears and take the appropriate precautions.

Remember, there are no hard and fast rules to ensure protection from a bear. Bear behavior differs under different conditions. A surprise encounter, particularly with a female bear and cubs, is dangerous. A normally placid mother may be quickly provoked if her cubs are disturbed, or if you come between her and the cubs.

Fresh bear tracks in the snow

If you see a bear, give it plenty of room. If it sees you, it will normally do the same thing. Do not make abrupt moves or noises that would startle the bear. Slowly detour, keeping upwind so it will get your scent and know you are there. If you can't detour, wait until the bear moves away from your route.

Keep in mind that you may be as much of a surprise to the bear as it is to you. On one occasion, I encountered a bear ambling down the trail toward me, oblivious to my presence. It was probably day dreaming about huckleberries. I softly whistled to get its attention, but I was downwind and it did not see me. Not wanting to shake hands, I spoke to get its attention. When it finally saw me, that bear was headed in the opposite direction as fast as it could go.

Should a bear charge you instead of running in the op-posite direction, head for the nearest tree tall enough to get you out of reach. Black bears can climb trees, but they can also be discouraged from doing so. Don't blindly run down the trail or into the brush. Bears can easily outrun humans and fleeing could help to excite the animal.

A clean campsite without tempting or strange odors will best ensure a night's sleep untroubled by bear visits. If you do not want a bear (or other animal) scavenging around your camp, do not leave food, toothpaste, or other attractive tidbits around camp or in fire rings while you are gone during the day, or while you are asleep at night. Also, do not take food to bed with you. Suspend food and garbage in sealed plastic bags at least 10 feet above the ground, 5 to 10 feet from the tree trunk, and 3 to 6 feet below the limb on which they hang.

You may be thinking that all this bear advice is actually for the birds. "There are no problem bears in the Mount Jefferson Wilderness," you say—at least not yet. But while writing this guide, I saw the tracks of a bear circle a lake. It had poked its nose into every fire ring, looking for food scraps. If you don't want bears in your camp, then you should follow common sense about camp cleanliness and hope that the person that used the camp ahead of you has done the same thing.

TRAIL ETIQUETTE

Horses have the right-of-way over hikers. Since horses cause more damage off the trail than hikers, hikers should step off the trail to let horses pass. Also, if horses or livestock should spook, it is best for the hiker to be off the trail rather than get run over. Speak to the horse and rider as soon as they are within distance. This will help to put the horse at ease.

Stand quietly while the horse passes. A bright pack, rattling cup or equipment can cause a horse to spook.

DOGS

The only dog that should be taken into the wilderness is one that does not bite, bark, chase animals, or range farther than 5 feet from its master. All other dogs should be left at home.

TRAILHEAD PARKING

It seems that a demented group of the public has taken to the sport of "car clouting" at many of the popular trailheads. While hikers are away in the woods, they drive to the trailhead parking area, smash the car windows, and leave. Often, they take valuables that are left in the cars.

According to the Forest Service, trailhead parking is unsupervised and at your own risk. When you leave your car, make sure it is locked and no valuables are in sight. Items such as cameras, firearms, radios, and hiking or climbing equipment should not be left behind. Your wallet, money, and keys are safest in your pocket or pack. If your vehicle is tampered with, you should report it to the County Sheriff's Department. If you are planning an extended trip, it is best to have someone drop you off and meet you when you return.

It is better to be safe than sorry.

Some Words on Wilderness Use

Llama packing—a new way to travel in the wilderness

PART 3:
Wilderness Attractions

WILDERNESS OUTFITTERS—HORSES AND LLAMAS

Many commercial guides, packers and outfitters lead trips into the Mount Jefferson Wilderness. If you do not relish the thought of packing five days' worth of food and gear on your back, having someone else do it is a pleasant idea indeed.

Llamas are fast becoming a popular alternative to horse packing. These docile and personable animals can carry twice as much as the typical backpacker, yet they leave little trace on the landscape compared to the much larger horse. Horses are voracious eaters requiring supplemental feed and hay—llamas require much less feed. A 2000-pound steel-shod horse will do much more damage to a trail or campsite than will the light hoof of a 200-pound llama. "Horse apples" on the trail are much more noticeable than the deer-like llama droppings. Except that you will have to hike and lead a llama instead of riding, llama packing offers all of the comforts of horse packing—a comfortable camp, good food and an easy pace. If you are interested in having someone pack you into the wilderness, you may want to consider llamas as an alternative to horses.

Appendix C contains a list of local commercial horse and llama packers who are registered with the Forest Service and who currently lead trips into the Mount Jefferson Wilderness. The listing of these packers does not constitute an endorsement of them over other organizations offering similar services.

The types of services offered include all-expense-paid trips, where the packer supplies all food and equipment for the length of the trip; spot pack trips, where the hiker and equipment are packed in and dropped off to be picked up at the end of the trip; and dunnage trips, where equipment is packed in to a predetermined camp and left to await the hikers' arrival. Inquire for specific information on the types of services offered.

FISHING

Fish are stocked in 86 lakes within the Mount Jefferson Wilderness. The Lake Tables describe each of the lakes which have been or are currently stocked with fish by the Oregon Fish and Wildlife Department. A popular fishing guide has been prepared for Oregon, and it gives additional information on many of the lakes included in the Lake Tables (see *References*).

A fishing license is reuqired and can be obtained from any sporting goods store. The fishing season is open through-out the year, although it is essentially limited to the periods when the area is free of snow. Numerous different species are stocked, and more than one species is often stocked in any particular lake. The use of rubber rafts is allowed on wilderness lakes.

Cleaning of fish within lakes or other bodies of water is prohibited, as is fishing in the outlet of Marion Lake or its tributaries. Anglers should consult the Oregon Sport Fishing Regulations for the most current information.

HUNTING

Hunting is allowed within the wilderness. Fortunately, the peak recreation season and the hunting seasons do not overlap. Therefore, there is little conflict between hunters and other recreationists.

The hunting season for deer, elk, and bear runs from early September through mid-November. Hikers and backpackers should wear distinctive and bright clothing if they enter the wilderness during hunting season.

Most hunting occurs south of Mount Jefferson, and often is associated with horse packing. Hunting does not usually occur around the more popular recreation areas, since the big game mammals tend to avoid them. Licenses are required and can be obtained from sporting goods stores. The Oregon Game Mammal Regulations should be consulted for specific information on each species.

TRAILS

There are over 200 miles of trails within the Mount Jefferson Wilderness. Each trail is different. Those constructed long ago may have a narrow tread, broken down with age and tending to get overgrown from disuse. Although more difficult, they often are covered with a carpet of moss and fir needles, allowing the hiker to approach animals silently. The more modern and heavily used trails have a wider tread, gentler grades, and conveniences such as bridges.

Trails aid travel in the wilderness, particularly in steep terrain, but don't feel you must only hike where the trails are shown on maps. Unmarked trails can be fun to hike and sometimes take you to the best camping and fishing spots. Whether you follow game trails, horse trails, or Indian trails, your trip will be filled with the kind of adventure you cannot get on maintained trails. If there are no trails, cross-country travel will get you there.

Pacific Crest Trail

The Pacific Crest Trail runs north and south through the full length of the Mount Jefferson Wilderness (36 miles). The original trail, known as the Oregon Skyline Trail, was under construction starting in the 1920's, and was completed by 1935. In 1968, the National Trails System Act officially designated the Pacific Crest National Scenic Trail. Since that time, new sections of the trail have been constructed, bypassing old sections such as the Hunt's Creek Trail 3440. The replacement trail from Cathedral Rocks to Milk Creek was constructed in the 1970's, and is one of the newest segments of the Pacific Crest Trail in the Wilderness.

This trail is constructed with a 24-inch-wide tread and a minimum of steep grades (generally, the steepest grades are less than 15 percent). It is popular with people who want to hike the length of Oregon, as well as those hardy individuals who try to make it all the way from Mexico to Canada. Consequently, you are likely to see a great number of hikers and horse packers along this route. Because the trail follows the Cascade crest, the camping spots are limited and often crowded. Water is not as readily available as along the lower slopes of the Cascades. Fishing is only possible if side trips are made to lower-elevation lakes.

Other Trails

Most of the other trails within the wilderness were originally constructed in the 1920's and 1930's for fire protection and the movement of grazing stock. Some of these trails are quite steep and definitely were not designed for the convenience of today's hiker. Nevertheless, they can be very enjoyable. The Trail Table and narrative included in each Area Discussion provide detailed information on all the trails which are currently on the Forest Service inventory.

Cross-Country Travel

This is what wilderness is all about. When Lewis and Clark came to Oregon and saw Mount Jefferson for the first time, there were no roads, no signs and no maps. They followed the route that made the most sense and experienced the sights and sounds of the true wilderness. While this may no longer be possible, cross-country travel offers the next best thing. It also helps to disperse the impact that hikers have on the wilderness, giving any one area more time to revegetate. All that is needed to get started is a map and compass (or an altimeter — see section on *Route Finding*).

MOUNTAIN CLIMBING

There are outstanding opportunities for mountain and rock climbing too numerous to mention in a general recreation guide such as this. Obviously, both Mount Jefferson and Three Fingered Jack are the principle climbing areas. On Three Fingered Jack alone, there are at least five established climbing routes, and many variations. For a more thorough discussion of climbing routes and areas, consult "A Climbing Guide to Oregon" or inquire with a climbing group such as the Santiam Alpine Club, Chemeketans, or the Mazamas (see *Appendix B*). Remember, climbers do not have privileges over and above other wilderness users. High camps are usually made in fragile alpine areas. Excessive use can be quite destructive. Climbing and descent routes can leave permanent scars on the face of the mountain.

Climbers can leave unwanted traces in the wilderness—here a climbing trail scars the mountainside

If all you would like to do is sit on a rock somewhere and watch climbers from a safe distance through a spotting scope, you should pick a location north or west of Mount Jefferson, or east of Three Fingered Jack, since these are the sides of the mountains with the most frequently climbed pinnacle routes.

There are numerous peaks, buttes and ridges that can be climbed without special equipment. All that is required are sturdy shoes and constitution. Marion Mountain, for instance, has a trail that leads to the top. Triangulation Peak, Bear Point, Grizzly Peak, and Maxwell Butte all have trails to the top, and all offer views equal to or better than those from the top of Mount Jefferson or Three Fingered Jack. The Triangulation Peak area has several rock pinnacles where technical rock climbing can be practiced only a short hike from the trailhead.

WINTER RECREATION

Winter is the time I enjoy the best, since remote areas of the wilderness are seldom if ever visited. Whether on skis or snow shoes, you have the freedom to go wherever you want. Most often, there are no trails to follow, since they are under several feet of snow, and blazes and signs are no longer visible. Snow conditions change daily, and what would be an easy ski one day, becomes an icy nightmare the next. For this reason, winter guides are impractical.

The winter use season generally extends from November 15 to April 15. During this period, travel throughout most of the wilderness is over snow. In the fall, users should be particularly aware that sudden snow storms can leave their cars stranded at the trailhead, many miles from a plowed highway.

By far, the most popular areas currently used for winter recreation are in the southern part of the area, including Maxwell Butte, Santiam Lake, Pacific Crest, and Summit Trails. If you don't want to see people, avoid these areas. Other areas which receive less use, include Big Meadows, and areas on the east side of the Pacific Crest. Obviously, areas which have good scenery in the summer will also be beautiful in the winter. It will just be colder.

WILD FLOWERS

Wild flowers can be seen throughout the wilderness, almost any time of year. However, a few places are noted for a greater than normal profusion of colorful flowers. If you are interested in observing flowers in the wilderness, these areas can be recommended. But do not think that these are the

Wilderness Attractions

only places with flowers; they grow everywhere.

You should not pick the flowers. If you must take something home with you, take a picture.

Location of Wild flower Displays

On the west side of the wilderness, the meadow areas in the Eight Lakes Basin and near Santiam and Duffy Lakes have flowers from July through August. Jefferson Park also has flowers, but high altitude and deeper snows make the season even later.

On the east side of the wilderness, you will find flowers along the summit trail in nearly all the meadows southeast of Three Fingered Jack. Canyon Creek Meadows is well known for its flower displays, a fact which accounts for a great deal of day-use in the area. The Brush Creek Trail has a good display of Washington (Santiam) Lilies, usually in August.

Huckleberries grow well along the Cabot Lake Trail. While they may not be much to look at, they sure taste good in pancakes. On the west side, the South Breitenbush Trail and Crown Lake areas also have good huckleberries.

Santiam (Washington) Lily

PART 4:
Area Discussions

Area Discussions

Mount Jefferson from a meadow off the Whitewater Trail

North Breitenbush Area

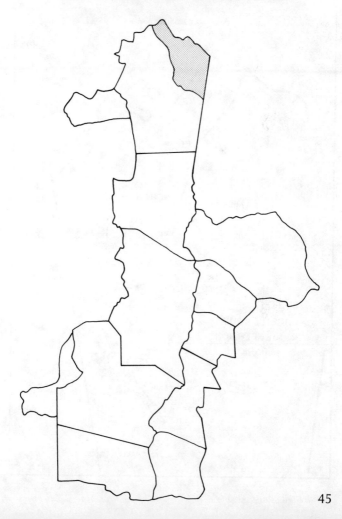

Area Discussions

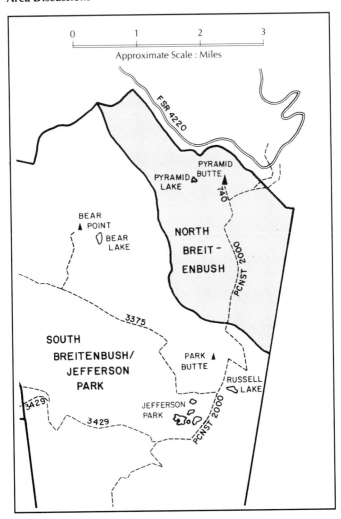

North Breitenbush Area

NORTH BREITENBUSH AREA

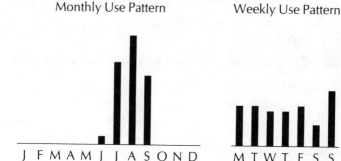

Monthly Use Pattern

Weekly Use Pattern

J F M A M J J A S O N D
Month

M T W T F S S
Day

This is the northernmost portion of the Mount Jefferson Wilderness, and one of the more popular entry points. Nine percent of all the people who enter the Mount Jefferson Wilderness do so via the Pacific Crest Trail passing through this area. However, less than 1 percent of all wilderness use actually occurs here, because most of the people pass through the area on their way to Jefferson Park.

There are two trail heads. The Pacific Crest Trail head actually begins on Road 4220, a quarter mile west of Breitenbush Lake. The other trailhead is located at Breitenbush Lake, where a portion of the old Oregon Skyline Trail leads into the wilderness. Both trails join at the wilderness boundary, where the permit box is located.

The name Breitenbush (for the river and the lake), comes from a pioneer hunter who lived on a tributary to the Santiam River. There are differing accounts of the man, one that he had one arm and his name was John Breitenbush. Another, that his name was actually Lewis Breitenbusher, a man who came to Oregon in 1849.

If you are seeking solitude when you enter this area, Pyramid, Davey, and Babe Lakes are good potential campsites. There are also a few campsites along the Pacific Crest Trail before it reaches the top of Park Ridge. However, you are likely to see many people on the trail.

The hike to the top of Park Ridge is well worth while, but somewhat steep and hazardous. The Pacific Crest Trail crosses Park Ridge at a very high and exposed location. Since mountain weather can change very rapidly, extra precaution should be taken to be well equipped when traveling this portion of the trail. From the top, you can see into Jefferson Park, a classic view seen in many photographs of the area. Look around, and you will see trees, few of which are more than 15 feet high, but which are as much as 150 years old. A large rock and mud flow can be seen on the east side of Jefferson Park. Reported to have surged down Mount Jefferson in 1934, it is a reminder that the process of erosion is still actively changing the alpine landscape.

If you do not wish to hike all the way to Park Ridge, a short hike up the Pyramid Trail 740, off the Pacific Crest Trail, offers another scenic view of the area. This used to be the site of a Forest Service lookout building, which has long since been removed. The trail to the top of the Butte is not recommended for horses.

Wild flowers bloom in late summer along the Pacific Crest Trail, particularly along the upper trail north of Park Ridge.

Mount Jefferson Wilderness Trails
North Breitenbush Area

Trail Name	Trail Number	Trail Dist. (Miles)	Elev. Gain (Feet)	Elev. Loss (Feet)	High Point (Feet)	Low Point (Feet)	Avg. Grade (%)	Max. Grade (%)	Access Trail Number
Pyramid Butte	740	0.5	315	0	6095	5780	12	20	2000
Pacific Crest	2000								—
Mt Hood NF Bdry to S-4220		4.8	0	1970	6910	5500	8	14	2000

Mount Jefferson Wilderness Lakes
North Breitenbush Area

Lake Name	Elev. (Feet)	Size (Acres)	Depth (Feet)	Fish Species	Number of Camp Sites	XC Miles From Trail	Access Trail Number	Miles From Trail Head
Davey	5200	2	14	CT	NS	0.5	Rd S-4220	0.5
Pyramid	5400	5	10	BT	3	0.7	Rd S-4220	0.7

NS = Not Surveyed
BT = Eastern Brook Trout

XC = Cross Country
RB = Rainbow Trout

CT = Cutthroat Trout

Distances to lakes are the shortest distance by the easiest route.
Access trails are listed in the order of travel to the lake.

49

Area Discussions

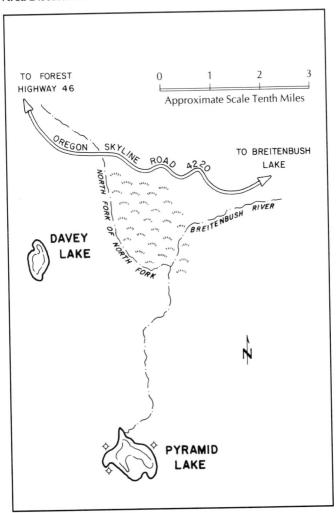

Davey and Pyramid Lakes Campsite Map

South Breitenbush/
Jefferson Park Area

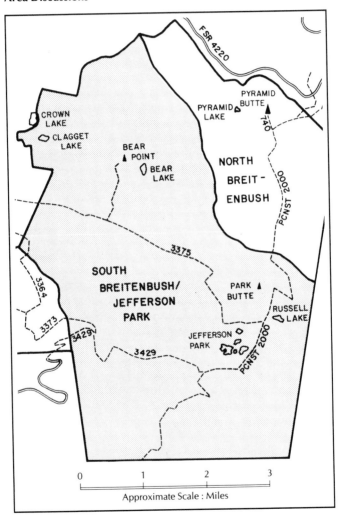

South Breitenbush/Jefferson Park Area

SOUTH BREITENBUSH/JEFFERSON PARK

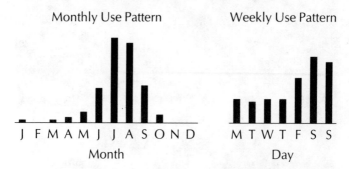

Monthly Use Pattern

J F M A M J J A S O N D
Month

Weekly Use Pattern

M T W T F S S
Day

The South Breitenbush area receives about 15,000 visitor-days of use each year—22 percent of all the use in the Mount Jefferson Wilderness. Except for the Marion Lake Basin area, it is the most heavily used area in the wilderness.

Access to the area is provided at eight entry points (trailheads). The most popular is the Whitewater Creek Trail 3429, which is used by more than 10 percent of all the people who enter the Mount Jefferson Wilderness. The Pacific Crest Trail is the next most popular—9 percent of the people entering the wilderness use this trail. The other six entry points are used by less than 3 percent of all visitors. They provide the best opportunities for hiking in solitude.

Long known for its scenic beauty, Jefferson Park attracts almost all the people who enter the South Breitenbush area. It is the single most popular destination in the wilderness, receiving 21 percent of all wilderness use. Two-fifths of all the people who go to Jefferson Park do so during August. It would not be unusual to find 500 people camped or roaming about Jefferson Park on a busy weekend. Obviously, camp-

A mist-shrouded pond in Jefferson Park

ing in Jefferson Park will have its rewards (outstanding scenery) and its drawbacks (notably, a lot of people, competition for campsites, scarce firewood, and a greater chance of contaminated water). There are good displays of wild flowers in all of the higher meadows and ridges in late summer.

Jefferson Park is the modern name for the area known to early explorers as "Hanging Valley"—an apt name for an area shaped by glaciers and left hanging as they retreated. Russell

Lake, the source of the South Fork Breitenbush River, was named for Dr. Israel C. Russell, an early geologist of the United States Geological Survey, who explored the area in the 1880's. In 1931, a group of boy scouts from Albany unknowingly gave the permanent name to Scout Lake, when they made a sign pointing to the lake they had camped at for several days. You only have to look at a map to figure out how Bays lake got its name.

If you must camp in Jefferson Park during August, you may still be able to avoid crowded camping if you camp away from the most popular lakes, such as Scout Lake with its 27 campsites. As can be seen in the campsite map, there are many areas within the park where camps with beautiful views can be made, if one is willing to hike a short distance to get drinking water. In the northwest corner of the park, many camps are available with ready access to water. Most people will not go more than 100 yards away from the popular lakes and the Pacific Crest Trail. When camping in little-used areas, do not make new fire rings unless absolutely necessary, and practice no-trace camping.

There is also a great deal of room for camping south of Russell Lake, with only a slightly greater distance needed for packing water. A snowmelt stream and small unnamed lakes southeast of Russell Lake can also accommodate dispersed camping since they are not within the Warm Springs Indian Reservation.

The area around Crown Lake and Clagget Lake is well suited to short one-day hikes and easy family camping trips. This area is also known as the "Firecamp Lakes" because it was a base camp for snag fallers after a fire swept through the area. The Crown Lake Trail 3362 starts at the end of Road 4685-330 and climbs up to Crown Lake. This is not a maintained Forest Service trail, and it is not shown on the Forest Service wilderness map. It is, however, shown on the more recent Detroit Ranger District maps. The trail is relatively steep compared to the Roaring Creek Trail 3361 which is the designated trail to Crown Lake. The Roaring Creek Trail also has more room for parking at the trailhead. Access to the other lakes in the area is achieved by hiking cross-country from Crown Lake.

The Craig Trail 3364 is remarkable, both for its precarious crossing of the South Breitenbush River on a downed tree, and an extremely long steep grade. In spite of the steep grade, the trail has an excellent tread. There are primitive camping sites near the junction with the Triangulation Trail 3373. The trail can also be used for a loop trip through Jefferson Park in combination with the South Breitenbush Trail 3375.

Mount Jefferson from Woodpecker Ridge

The Woodpecker Ridge Trail 3442 is a little-used alternate access to the Pacific Crest Trail and to Jefferson Park. There are campsites available at an unnamed lake along the Pacific Crest Trail, approximately 0.3 miles northeast of the Wood-pecker Trail junction. Also, there are several campsites just off the Pacific Crest Trail, on a bench overlooking the Russell Creek valley, approximately 0.3 miles south of of where the trail crosses Russell Creek. Approximately 0.2 miles north of the Russell Creek crossing, there are several campsites west of the trail in a stand of large timber.

Caution should be used when crossing Russell Creek in the spring. Each year, a snow bridge forms when spring snowmelt undermines the packed snow crossing. This snow bridge could give way without warning. To avoid this haz-ard, if it exists, cross the snow as far upstream as possible.

The South Breitenbush Trail is probably the most under-rated trail in the wilderness. While parts are rough and rocky, it offers a peaceful entry into Jefferson Park without climbing over Park Ridge or jostling with horses and hikers up the Pacific Crest Trail or the Whitewater Trail. There are several campsites along the South Breitenbush Trail, starting approx-imately 0.5 miles east of the junction with the Bear Point Trail 3342, and continuing all the way to Jefferson Park. Primitive camps with good views can be made west of the trail in the northwest end of Jefferson Park. The small cabin located along the trail (approximately 0.4 miles before the Bear Point Trail 3342 junction) was used to store tree seed-lings for replanting, after the area was swept by the Firecamp Lakes fire.

The Bear Point Trail 3342 is reached via the South Breiten-bush Trail. It is steep, but rises to a commanding view of the

The remains of a seedling shack used to plant trees after a fire

entire Cascade range. The hike is well worth the effort. In the fall, this trail and the South Breitenbush Trail 3375 both provide access to good huckleberry picking areas.

Off the beaten path in the South Breitenbush area, you can find Mildred, Slideout, Swindle, Bear and Whitewater Lakes. They are all stocked with fish, yet receive comparative little, if any, use because of the lack of direct trail access. Mildred, Slideout, Swindle and Bear lakes can be reached by traveling cross-country from Crown Lake. Whitewater Lake can be reached by traveling cross-country from Forest Service Road 2243, or from the Pacific Crest Trail.

Mount Jefferson Wilderness Trails
South Breitenbush/Jefferson Park Area

Trail Name	Trail Number	Trail Dist. (Miles)	Elev. Gain (Feet)	Elev. Loss (Feet)	High Point (Feet)	Low Point (Feet)	Avg. Grade (%)	Max. Grade (%)	Access Trail Number
Bear Point	3342	1.8	1683	0	6043	4360	18	20	3375
Roaring Creek	3361	0.9	200	70	4920	4720	6	16	3361
Crown Lake	3362	0.5	352	0	4852	4500	13	13	3362
Craig	3364	2.7	1900	240	4900	3000	15	18	3364
South Breitenbush	3375	6.5	3110	350	6050	3120	10	17	3375
Whitewater	3429	4.2	1360	0	5560	4200	6	13	3429
Pacific Crest	2000								—
Milk Cr to Mt Hood NF Bdry		8.5	2750	270	6910	4300	7	12	3429/3440/ 3442

Mount Jefferson Wilderness Lakes
South Breitenbush/Jefferson Park Area

Lake Name	Elev. (Feet)	Size (Acres)	Depth (Feet)	Fish Species	Number of Camp Sites	XC Miles From Trail	Access Trail Number	Miles From Trail Head
Bays	6000	12	20	BT	17	1.5	3429/2000	5.7
Bear	5260	9	24	BT	4	2.5	3361	3.5
Claggett	4920	6	10	BT	8	0.3	3361	1.3
Crown	4852	12	6	RB	10	—	3361	1.0
Mildred	4880	3	11	BT	3	2.0	3361	3.0
Park	5800	2	8	BT	16	0.1	3375	5.6
Rock	5850	2	10	BT	9	0.3	3429/2000	5.8
Russel	5866	7	27	CT	26	0.1	2000	5.7
Scout	5820	7	31	BT	27	0.1	3429/2000	5.5
Sheep	4930	2	18	BT	2	0.5	3361	1.5
Slideout	4740	6	18	BT	3	2.3	3361	3.3
Swindle	4960	3	NS	BT	NS	2.0	3361	3.0
Whitewater	4200	3	12	CT	NS	1.0	Rd 2243-375	1.0

NS = Not Surveyed XC = Cross Country CT = Cutthroat Trout
BT = Eastern Brook Trout RB = Rainbow Trout

Distances to lakes are the shortest distance by the easiest route.
Access trails are listed in the order of travel to the lake.

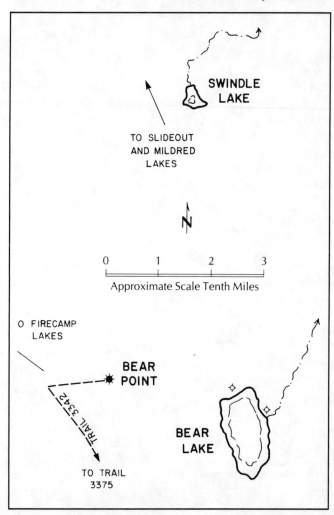

SWINDLE LAKE

TO SLIDEOUT
AND MILDRED
LAKES

N

0   1   2   3

Approximate Scale Tenth Miles

O FIRECAMP
LAKES

**BEAR
POINT**

TRAIL 3342

**BEAR
LAKE**

TO TRAIL
3375

Bear and Swindle Lakes Campsite Map   61

Area Discussions

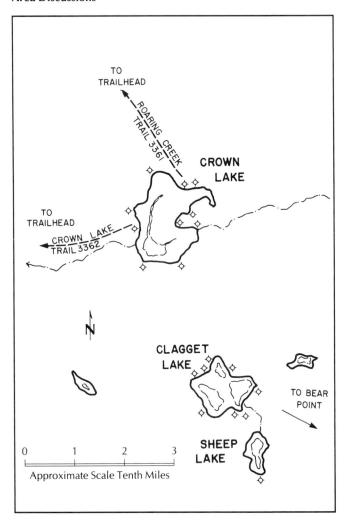

TO
TRAILHEAD

ROARING CREEK
TRAIL 3361

CROWN
LAKE

TO
TRAILHEAD

CROWN LAKE
TRAIL 3362

N

CLAGGET
LAKE

TO BEAR
POINT

SHEEP
LAKE

0   1   2   3
Approximate Scale Tenth Miles

Firecamp Lakes Campsite Map

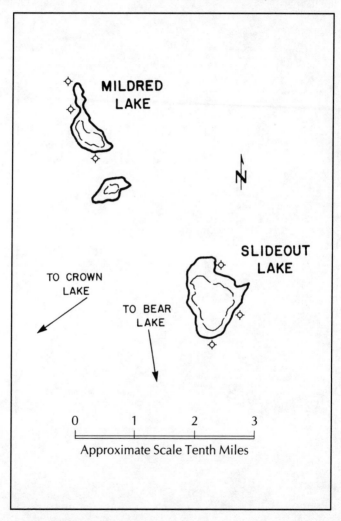

MILDRED
LAKE

N

SLIDEOUT
LAKE

TO CROWN
LAKE

TO BEAR
LAKE

0   1   2   3
Approximate Scale Tenth Miles

Mildred and Slideout Lakes Campsite Map   63

Area Discussions

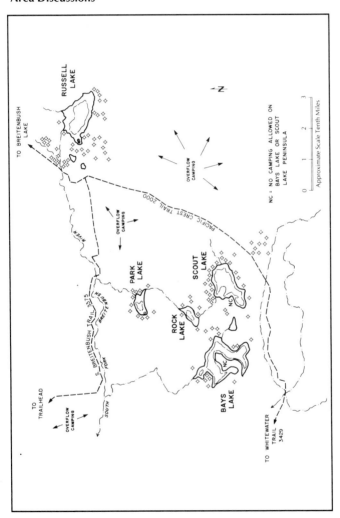

Jefferson Park Campsite Map

Pamelia Creek Basin Area

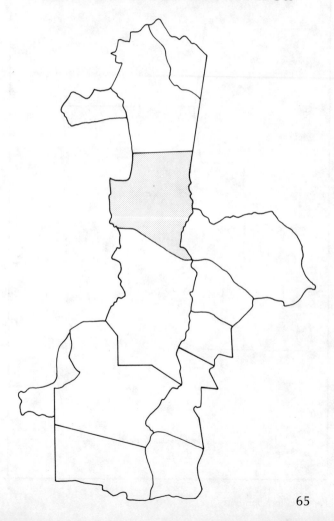

Area Discussions

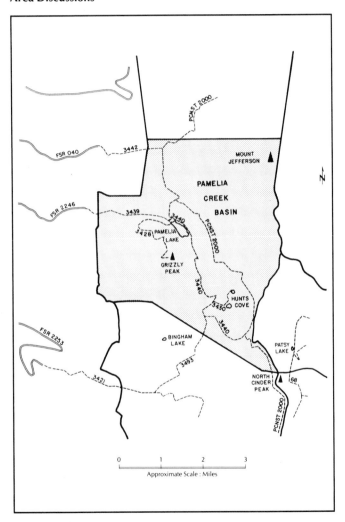

Pamelia Creek Basin Area

PAMELIA CREEK BASIN

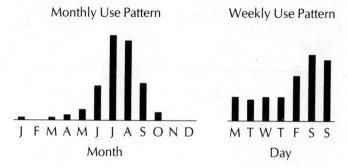

Monthly Use Pattern

Weekly Use Pattern

J F M A M J J A S O N D
Month

M T W T F S S
Day

   The Pamelia Creek Basin area receives about 10,000 visitor-days of use each year—17 percent of all the use in the Mount Jefferson Wilderness. It is the third most heavily used area in the wilderness.

   Access to the area is provided at two entry points. The most popular is the Pamelia Creek Trail 3439, which is traveled by 18 percent of all the people who enter the wilderness. On a busy weekend, as many as 300 people may head up this one trail. The other access, the Woodpecker Ridge Trail 3442, receives virtually no use, despite the short distance to the Pacific Crest Trail.

   Almost all the use in the Pamelia Creek Basin is concentrated at two areas—Pamelia Lake and Hunt's Cove. A busy weekend would find up to 200 people crowded around the north and east shore of Pamelia Lake, since this is the only place where camps can be made. Up to another 100 people could be found at Hunt's and Hank's Lakes. As a single destination point, Pamelia Lake is the third most popular area in the wilderness, while Hunt's Cove is the sixth most popular. Needless to say, if you avoid these two areas, you will see very few people.

The use at Pamelia Lake is almost evenly distributed between the months of July and August. Hunt's Cove, because of its higher elevation, receives the greatest share of use in August. As is the case in most of the wilderness, the late fall months are much less crowded.

Pamelia Creek was named by the Marion County road surveyor John Minto for Pamelia Ann Berry, a girl who cooked for the survey crew. Pamelia Lake was later named for the creek, presumably by Judge John B. Waldo, who spent much time in the Cascades. Waldo later was honored by giving his name to a glacier on the south side of Mount Jefferson.

The Pamelia Lake Trail 3439 is relatively low in elevation and is clear of snow much earlier than almost any other area in the Mount Jefferson Wilderness. As a result, it receives

Pamelia Lake

Mushrooms abound along the Pamelia Lake Trail

very high use from May through August. This trail is particularly noted for the "rain forest" type canopy of dense old growth trees. In the fall, there is an abundant growth of mushrooms. (Note: Some mushrooms are extremely poisonous. You should not eat any wild mushroom unless it has been identified by someone who knows what they are doing.)

There are no alternate camp sites around Pamelia Lake. If you camp here during the peak of the season, you will just have to make the best of the sites available as shown on campsite map. There are several campsites along Pamelia Creek before you reach the lake, and a few more sites along Hunts Creek south of the lake, but not many.

If you intend to camp at Hunt's Cove during the peak of the season, there are a few alternate camp sites on a bench overlooking a meadow before you reach the lakes. Also, there are several open areas and flat spots farther up the basin

Area Discussions

Falls on Hunt's Creek

southeast of the lakes. Water is available from seasonal streams. The upper Hunt's Cove basin is the site of early sheep camps, when the high country was extensively used for summer pasture. Now, the area is used primarily by deer, elk and bear, and is a popular area for deer hunters during the early Cascades season.

One special feature you should not miss is a water fall on Hunt's Creek, just off the Hunt's Creek Trail 3440. Watch for an informal trail leading off the main trail at a switchback near the 4900 foot contour.

If you follow the Hunt's Creek Trail 3440 all the way to the end, you will reach a junction with the Pacific Crest Trail. (How many switchbacks did you count on the way up from the Hunt's Cove Trail?) This junction is incorrectly shown on the Forest Service wilderness map at an elevation of 6060 feet, when it is actually in a saddle at elevation 5900 feet. You will find that several old sheep and stock trails fan out in

Hunt's Cove from upper Hunt's Creek Trail

71

Trail junction sign near Milk Creek

different directions at the junction. Since they can be confused with Forest Service trails, check your directions carefully, and make sure you are on the correct trail when leaving the area. The trail junction sign was not adequate in 1982. If you should choose to follow the informal trails, instead of the Forest Service trails, they will lead you to several small lakes and open areas suitable for camping. Some of these sites have excellent views of the Cascade Range to the south.

Older maps do not show that the Pacific Crest Trail has been rerouted past Cathedral Rocks, Shale Lake, and then down to a junction with the Hunt's Creek Trail 3440 at Milk Creek. The current Forest Service wilderness map does show the new route of the trail, but it incorrectly shows the distance of this leg as 4.8 miles, when it is actually 6.5 miles.

When hiking the Pacific Crest Trail to Shale Lake, be aware that the trail goes directly to the lake instead of passing southwest of the lake as shown on the Forest Service map

Mount Jefferson from Grizzly Peak

(see campsite map). Alternate camps can be made at numerous open areas and small lakes to the east of Shale Lake, should it be crowded when you arrive. Remember Shale Lake is on the Pacific Crest Trail and is a major stopping place.

There are a few informal places to camp near the junction of the Pacific Crest Trail and the Hunt's Creek Trail in the Milk Creek Valley. The area has nice views of Mount Jefferson. If you camp here, you may want to climb to a vantage point to observe the tremendous debris flow which cascaded over the upper ridges and down the valley wiping out all the vegetation in its path. The valley is now littered with the debris from this flow, which may have occurred when water breached a moraine dam formed by the Milk Creek glacier, or when a snow avalanche broke loose from the upper ridges. Even though the vegetation is recovering, the debris path is still quite evident.

Area Discussions

A hike up the Grizzly Peak Trail 3428 will reward you with a commanding view of the Hunt's Creek basin and Pamelia Lake. There are no existing campsites along the trail, but there are some flat areas near the 5200 foot contour where camps could be made. Water is seasonal.

Sometimes it helps to change your perspective and focus in on the small parts of the wilderness—here a spider on Grizzly Peak

Mount Jefferson Wilderness Trails
Pamelia Creek Basin Area

Trail Name	Trail Number	Trail Dist. (Miles)	Elev. Gain (Feet)	Elev. Loss (Feet)	High Point (Feet)	Low Point (Feet)	Avg. Grade (%)	Max. Grade (%)	Access Trail Number
Grizzly Peak	3428	3.0	1909	0	5799	3890	12	18	3439
Hunt's Cove	3430	0.8	295	70	5235	5010	9	16	3439/3440
Pamelia Lake	3439	2.4	640	0	3940	3300	5	5	3439
Hunt's Creek	3440	6.8	2230	650	6030	3900	8	16	3439
Woodpecker	3442	1.8	820	220	5090	4450	11	18	3442
Pacific Crest	2000								—
Cathedral Rocks to Milk Cr		6.5	0	1600	5900	4300	5	9	3440

Mount Jefferson Wilderness Lakes
Pamelia Creek Basin Area

Lake Name	Elev. (Feet)	Size (Acres)	Depth (Feet)	Fish Species	Number of Camp Sites	XC Miles From Trail	Access Trail Number	Miles From Trail Head
Coyote	5900	1	12	CT	3	0.1	3439/3440/2000	7.8
Hank's	5144	7	12	BT,RB	7	—	3439/3440/3430	5.7
Hunt's	5236	7	13	RB,CT	4	—	3439/3440/3430	6.1
Pamelia	3884	45	12	CT	72	—	3439	2.2
Shale	5900	1	14	BT	10	—	3439/3440/2000	7.7

NS = Not Surveyed
BT = Eastern Brook Trout

XC = Cross Country
RB = Rainbow Trout

CT = Cutthroat Trout

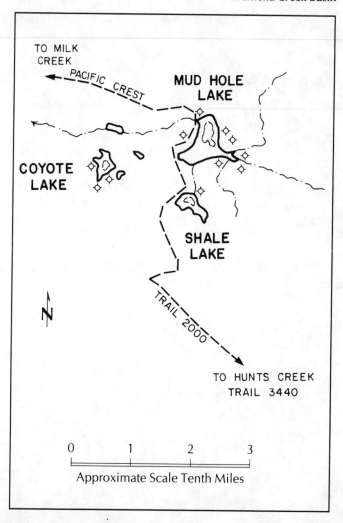

TO MILK
CREEK

PACIFIC CREST

MUD HOLE
LAKE

COYOTE
LAKE

SHALE
LAKE

N

TRAIL 2000

TO HUNTS CREEK
TRAIL 3440

0 1 2 3

Approximate Scale Tenth Miles

Shale Lake Area Campsite Map

Area Discussions

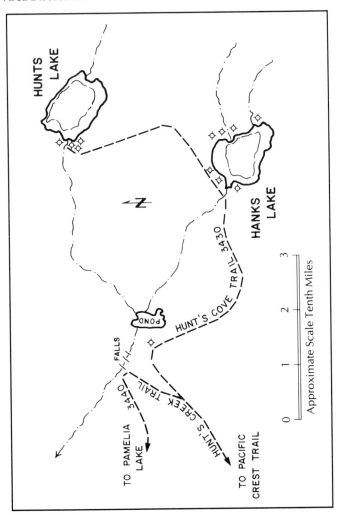

Hunts Cove Campsite Map

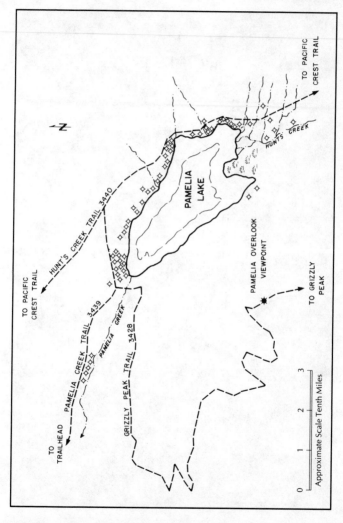

Pamelia Lake Campsite Map

Area Discussions

Marion Lake Trail—the most heavily used trail in the wilderness

Marion Lake Basin Area

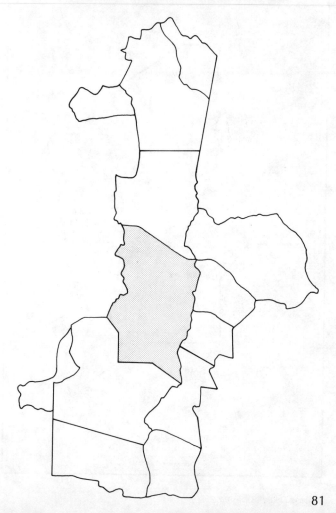

Area Discussions

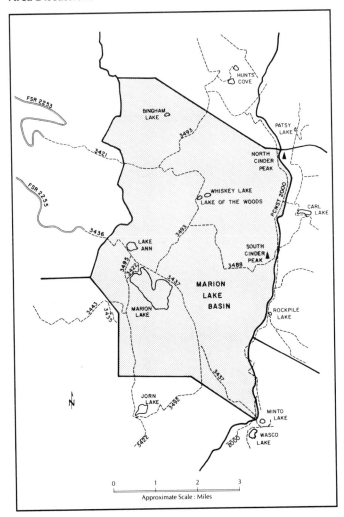

Marion Lake Basin Area

MARION LAKE BASIN

Monthly Use Pattern

Weekly Use Pattern

J F M A M J J A S O N D

M T W T F S S

Month

Day

The Marion Lake Basin area receives about 15,000 visitor-days of use each year—24 percent of all the wilderness use. This is the most frequently visited area in the wilderness.

Access is provided at two entry points, and as in the Pamelia Creek Basin area, one trail is very heavily used while the other receives very little use. The Marion Creek Trail 3436 is the most popular. More than 25 percent of all the people who enter the Mount Jefferson Wilderness do so on this trail—as many as 300 to 400 people on a busy weekend. Now you know why the trail is more than 3 feet wide. It has to be to keep people from trampling each other. The parking situation at the trail head is far from ideal. On the busiest weekends, the lot is full to overflowing and cars are parked more than 1/4 mile down the road.

In contrast, the Bingham Ridge Trail 3421, the other entry point into the area, is used by less than 1 percent of all people entering the wilderness, and most of this use occurs during the hunting season.

Virtually all use in the Marion basin occurs at Marion Lake and Ann Lake. At Marion Lake alone, there are over 100 established campsites, with well over 250 people camped around the lake on a busy weekend. The total amount of use at the lake is second only to that in Jefferson Park.

At 360 acres, Marion Lake is the largest in the wilderness. Because it is relatively low in elevation (4130 feet) and close to the trailhead (2 miles), the area is used almost continually throughout the five-month-long summer recreation season. The greatest use occurs in July and August, but May, June, and September also see a lot of visitors.

Overnight camping is very popular at Marion Lake. Most people camp on the north and west side of the lake. Therefore, if you must go to Marion Lake during the busy season and you cannot find a campsite immediately, your best bet is to head toward the south and east ends of the lake (see campsite map). These campsites are used relatively infrequently, and offer good views of Mount Jefferson. An informal trail which goes all the way around the lake can be used to get to these more remote sites. Unfortunately, Horse Pasture Creek is quite deep where it flows into the lake and there are no fallen trees big enough to cross. Wading is the best way to cross if you intend to circle the lake.

Camping is not allowed within 100 feet of the lakeshore, anywhere around the lake. There is one area along the west shore where camps have been made closer than 100 feet in the past. Camping at these sites is now prohibited. Camping is also not allowed on the Peninsula, a small rocky point at the west end of the lake. Sanitation has become a problem in this area due to the excessive and continual use that it received prior to being closed to camping. Wilderness Rangers will require you to move camp if you are camped in a restricted area. So, if you are not fond of setting up camp more than once a day, it would be advisable to camp only where it is allowed.

About the Wilderness Rangers. These dedicated Forest Service employees are on duty patrolling the wilderness to ensure that the rules and regulations are followed. They are assigned to patrol the most heavily used areas where overuse can lead to damage of the wilderness resource. As you might imagine, since Marion Lake is the second most heavily used area in the wilderness, it is regularly patrolled by the Forest Service. Most of us can accept the fact that some form of regulation and monitoring of wilderness use is necessary to ensure that the wilderness is a pleasant and beautiful place to visit. However, if you are the type who does not like being supervised by the government, then you should consider camping somewhere else. For example, alternative camp-sites are located approximately 1 mile south of Marion Lake, along the Blue Lake Trail 3422. Several campsites can be found at the small lake near the junction with the Pine Ridge Trail 3443, and there is a lot of flat ground for extra camps nearby. Both Jenny Lake and Melis Lake offer secluded camping only a short distance off the trail.

Marion Lake has long been a center of activity and a major attraction, even before the area was included in the Mount Jefferson Wilderness. A Forest Service guard station once stood near the junction of Marion Lake Trail 3436 and the Blue Lake Trail 3422. Many boats used to be stored at the lake all year. In the spring, fishermen would dig them out of the snow and use them to reach the deeper parts of the lake. Even today, many people pack in rubber rafts for fishing. On the north side of the lake, Dr. A. G. Prill had a summer cabin which he would occupy many months of the year. A noted amateur naturalist, Prill spent long hours studying the birds of Oregon. His collection of birds and eggs is on display at the University of Oregon. A small lake north of Marion Lake was named after Dr. Prill. After designation of the Mount Jefferson Wilderness, the Forest Service removed both the guard station and the Prill cabin, as they were judged incompatible with wilderness use. Today, all that remains of the Prill cabin is the fireplace hearth on the north side of the Minto Pass Trail 3437, about 0.5 miles from the junction with the Lake of the Woods Trail 3493.

Below Marion Lake, Marion Creek cascades over picturesque falls, sometimes referred to as Gatch Falls. They are named Marion Falls on the Forest Service wilderness map. To get to the falls, look for informal trails leading west off the Marion Outlet Trail 3495, down to the creek.

The remainder of the Marion basin away from Marion Lake receives only 3 percent of all the use in the Mount Jefferson Wilderness. Included in this area are 12 lakes which are stocked with fish. The Bingham Ridge Trail 3421

Puncheon bridges have been constructed in some areas to minimize impact to wet areas

Mount Jefferson from South Cinder Peak

is an excellent way to reach most of these lakes, including those in the remote and virtually untouched upper Whiskey Creek basin (see campsite map). Topographically, this is perhaps the most complex and interesting area in the wilderness, being patterned throughout with meadows, lakes and ridges. This area can also be reached by descending from the Pacific Crest Trail north of South Cinder Peak.

The Bingham Ridge Trail 3421 can also be the start of a loop hike to the Pacific Crest Trail via the Lake of the Woods Trail 3493, the Swallow Lake Trail 3488, and the Hunt's Creek Trail 3440. Some of the trail is quite steep, but in exchange for your effort, you will be rewarded by not seeing many people. Campsites can be found along this route about 1 mile from the Bingham Ridge trailhead, along the Lake of the Woods Trail where it crosses the outlet from Swallow Lake, along the Minto Pass Trail where it crosses the north fork of Horse Pasture Creek, and farther along this same trail, toward the Pacific Crest Trail, near some small ponds and meadows.

John Minto and his Marion County road survey crew also named Marion Lake. The name they selected was that of General Francis Marion (the Swamp Fox) who served in the Revolutionary War. His exploits were popularized in a book widely read by early Oregon settlers.

The name for Swallow Lake, on the other hand, has a somewhat clouded history. The most common story tells of how John Swallow, a sheepherder, drowned in the lake. Friends found the body and started to pack it out, but the state of decomposition was more than they could bear. After a short distance, they gave up, burying Swallow near what was then the Skyline Trail. His grave can still be seen today, only a few feet off the Lake of the Woods Trail 3493, near the junction with the Swallow Lake Trail 3488.

Mount Jefferson Wilderness Trails
Marion Lake Basin Area

Trail Name	Trail Number	Trail Dist. (Miles)	Elev. Gain (Feet)	Elev. Loss (Feet)	High Point (Feet)	Low Point (Feet)	Avg. Grade (%)	Max. Grade (%)	Access Trail Number
Bingham Ridge	3421	3.4	1210	50	5360	4200	7	19	3421
Blue Lake	3422	7.6	1500	880	5350	4140	6	18	3436
Marion Lake	3436	2.6	940	0	4300	3360	7	12	3436
Minto Pass	3437	4.7	1240	150	5390	4150	6	20	3436
Swallow Lake	3488	3.6	1620	110	6330	4750	9	28	3436
Lake of the Woods	3493	5.9	1435	395	5460	4280	6	20	3436
Marion Outlet	3495	0.6	90	0	4130	4040	3	6	3436
Pacific Crest	2000								–
Porkupine Rdg to Cathedral R.		13.0	1460	2040	6480	5300	5	12	65/3437

Mount Jefferson Wilderness Lakes
Marion Lake Basin Area

Lake Name	Elev. (Feet)	Size (Acres)	Depth (Feet)	Fish Species	Number of Camp Sites	XC Miles From Trail	Access Trail Number	Miles From Trail Head
Ann	4000	16	10	BT	7	—	3436	1.4
Bigfoot*	5840	2	20	BT	NS	1.9	3436/3493	7.0
Bingham	4700	4	4	CT	NS	0.7	3421/3493	4.8
Enelrad*	5520	2	15	CT	NS	1.4	3436/3493	6.2
Lake of the Woods	4850	5	9	RB	5	—	3436/3493	5.0
Marion	4130	360	180	BT,RB, CT	115	—	3436	2.1

Lake							
Melis	4800	5	17	BT	3	0.2	3436/3495/3422	4.9
Midget	4750	1	4	–	2	–	3436/3493	4.4
Papoose	5320	1	NS	–	1	–	3421/3493	5.0
Prill	5140	8	24	BT	6	1.2	3436/3493	4.4
Sad	5100	2	10	BT	NS	0.3	3436/3493/3488	4.7
Sitton*	5760	2	15	RB	NS	0.6	3436/3493	5.4
Swallow	5300	2	13	BT	10	–	3436/3493/3488	6.2
Junction Pond*	4700	1	NS	–	3	–	3436/3495/3422	4.0
Whiskey	4950	3	12	BT	4	0.3	3436/3493	5.3

NS = Not Surveyed   XC = Cross Country

BT = Eastern Brook Trout   RB = Rainbow Trout   CT = Cutthroat Trout

indicates that the lake name does not appear on most maps
Distances to lakes are the shortest distance by the easiest route.
Access trails are listed in the order of travel to the lake.

Area Discussions

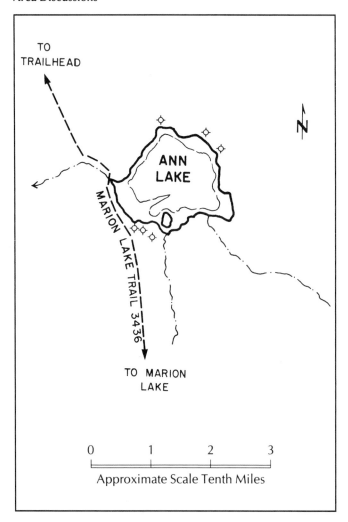

TO
TRAILHEAD

N

ANN
LAKE

MARION LAKE TRAIL 3436

TO MARION
LAKE

| 0 | 1 | 2 | 3 |

Approximate Scale Tenth Miles

Ann Lake Campsite Map

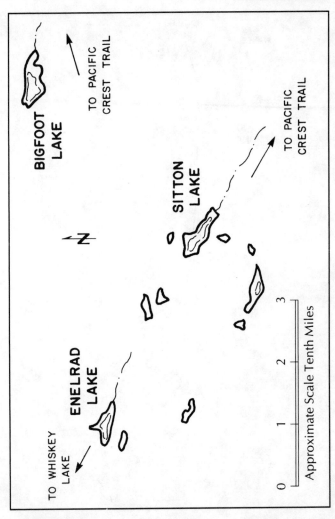

Area Discussions

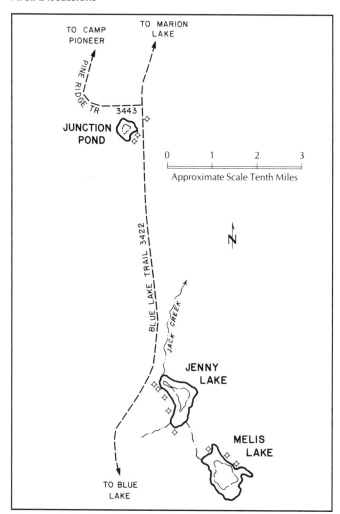

Jenny and Melis Lakes Campsite Map

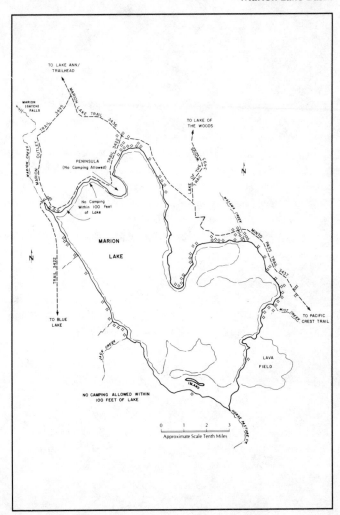

Marion Lake Campsite Map

Area Discussions

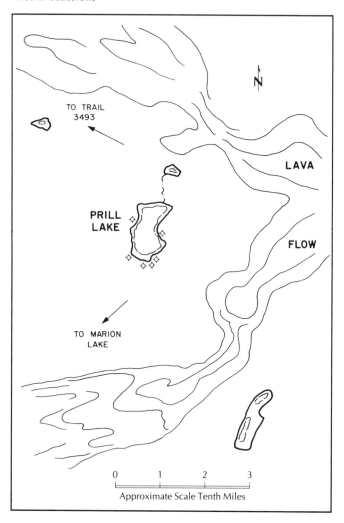

Prill Lake Campsite Map

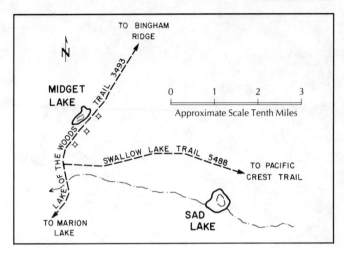

Midget Lake Campsite Map

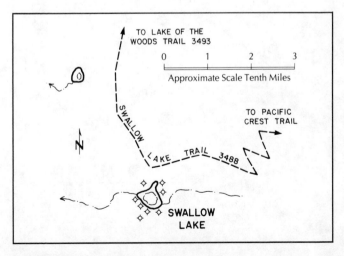

Swallow Lake Campsite Map

Area Discussions

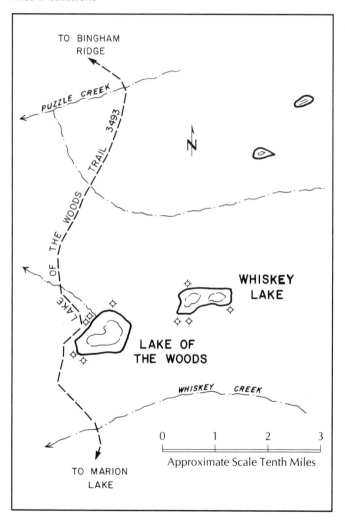

Whiskey Lake and Lake of the Woods Campsite Map

Santiam/Eight Lakes Basin Area

Area Discussions

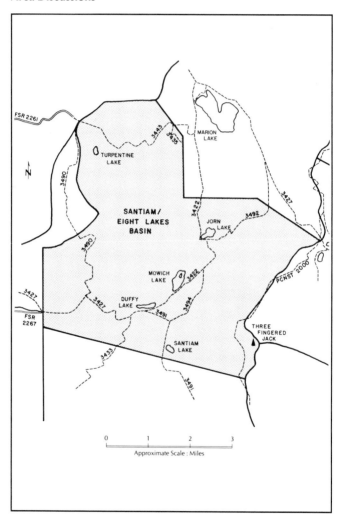

Santiam/Eight Lakes Basin Area

SANTIAM/EIGHT LAKES BASIN

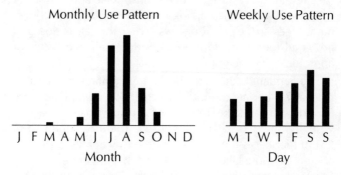

Monthly Use Pattern

J F M A M J J A S O N D
Month

Weekly Use Pattern

M T W T F S S
Day

The Santiam/Eight Lakes Basin area is the third most popular area in the wilderness. It receives 20 percent of all wilderness use. Unlike the Pamelia Creek and Marion Lake Basin areas, where almost all the use is concentrated at two major lakes, the use in this area is spread out between several popular destinations. For example, the Eight Lakes Basin, Mowich Lake, Duffy Lake and Santiam Lake account for 7, 2, 7, and 3 percent of the total wilderness use respectively. The peak season for all these lakes occurs in August. Santiam Lake, for instance, receives one-half of all use in August.

There are two main entry points into the area. The Duffy Lake Trail 3427 is the most popular access—7 percent of all visitors entering the wilderness do so by this route. The other access, the Pine Ridge Trail 3443, is used by less than 2 percent of all wilderness visitors. You can also get to several of the lakes by traveling through the Maxwell Butte area to the south, or the Marion Basin area to the north.

The Pine Ridge Trail starts at the Camp Pioneer parking lot. Sometimes the road is closed by a gate 0.2 miles west of the

Area Discussions

parking lot, to discourage vandalism at the Boy Scout camp. An alternate trail access has been constructed approximately 0.7 miles west of the parking lot, in order to allow convenient access to the Pine Ridge Trail when the gate is closed. A new trail then leads to the Pine Ridge Trail, a distance of approximately one mile.

The Santiam/Eight Lakes Basin area contains more lakes than any other area in the wilderness (34 named lakes are included in the Lake Tables). As a result, many areas are virtually unexplored and little used. The area southeast of Camp Pioneer is mostly used by the Boy Scouts and a few anglers. Remote lakes like Green Peak and Grenet get very little use. Other lakes are just off the beaten path, but because the trail passes them by, they get little use as well. These include the Cincha Lakes, Latigo and Alforja Lakes, and several other small lakes south of Duffy Lake. These are all stocked with fish and well worth a visit. The name Latigo

Bowerman Lake

Three Fingered Jack from South Cinder Peak

comes from a Spanish word "whip," which in America means saddle strap.

A major error in the Forest Service wilderness map occurs at the junction of the Duffy Lake Trail 3427 and the Turpentine Trail 3490. The junction actually occurs approximately 0.4 miles west of the point shown on the map, at an elevation of approximately 4460 feet. (This may be part of the reason why many people do not find Cincha and Little Cincha Lakes.)

If you decide to use the more popular lakes during the peak of the season, you should be prepared for crowded conditions. There are virtually no other campsites at Mowich Lake other than those shown in campsite map. Other lakes have some potential for overflow camps. For example, additional camp spots can be made south of Duffy Lake, Jorn Lake, and Bowerman Lake, in any of several open areas. There is also plenty of extra room to the northeast of Santiam

Lake. Even so, your best bet is to try to avoid the crowded areas altogether, then settle back and enjoy the solitude of the backcountry. Why go to all the trouble to plan and pack for a trip, only to have it spoiled by too many people?

While most of the camping opportunities are around lakes, there are some additional areas where camps can be made. Along the Turpentine Trail 3490, there are opportunities to camp at Swede Creek and in small meadow areas near Green Creek. Along the Bowerman Lake Trail 3492, there are some flat areas suitable for camping, south of the intersection with the Minto Pass Trail 3437. Seasonal water can be found farther south.

Santiam Lake is the headwaters of the North Santiam River. It derives its name from the Santiam Indians who lived near the river in the Willamette Valley. Just north of the lake, you can actually jump across the river when it is not too high, but this is one of the last places you can do so. The river must be forded during high water (early summer and late fall) where it is crossed by the Lava Trail 3435 and the Duffy Trail 3427. The best way to negotiate these troublesome crossings is to use a pair of sneakers to protect tender feet and a stout stick for balance. Teetering on slippery boulders and logs can sometimes result in an unwanted bath.

The short trip up the Marion Mountain Trail 3435 offers more than a spectacular view of Marion Lake and Mount Jefferson. The steady grade and good tread make for a relatively easy walk. Some camps have been made at the summit in some relatively level areas. There will not be any water except for patches of snow early in the year.

Mount Jefferson Wilderness Trails
Santiam/Eight Lakes Basin Area

Trail Name	Trail Number	Trail Dist. (Miles)	Elev. Gain (Feet)	Elev. Loss (Feet)	High Point (Feet)	Low Point (Feet)	Avg. Grade (%)	Max. Grade (%)	Access Trail Number
Blue Lake	3422	7.6	1500	880	5350	4140	6	18	3436
Duffy Lake	3427								
Duffy Lake (Main)		3.7	800	0	4800	4000	4	13	3427
Lava	3433	2.9	380	320	5140	4780	5	18	3427
Marion Mountain	3435	0.8	491	0	5351	4860	11	19	3443
Pine Ridge	3443	4.4	525	375	4880	4460	4	6	3443
Pine Ridge Alt	3443	1.3	440	0	4600	4160	7	7	3443A
Turpentine	3490	5.6	920	750	5160	4280	6	22	3443
Santiam	3491	4.4	485	505	5420	5050	4	18	2000
Bowerman Lake	3492	3.3	570	40	5120	4550	3	20	3436
Dixie Lakes	3494	1.5	430	20	5380	4950	6	11	3427
Pacific Crest	2000								—
Porkupine Rdg to Cathedral R.		13.0	1460	2040	6480	5300	5	12	65/3437

Area Discussions

Mount Jefferson Wilderness Lakes
Santiam/Eight Lakes Basin Area

Lake Name	Elev. (Feet)	Size (Acres)	Depth (Feet)	Fish Species	Number of Camp Sites	XC Miles From Trail	Access Trail Number	Miles From Trail Head
Alforja	4700	4	5	BT	1	0.2	3427	2.2
Alice	5350	1	9	BT	3	–	3427/3422	5.6
Blue	5350	10	40	BT	13	–	3436/3495/3422	6.4
Bowerman	5050	5	10	BT	5	0.1	3427/3422/3492	7.0
Cincha	4560	2	7	BT	1	0.1	3427	2.0
Chiquito	4800	7	22	BT	5	0.4	3436/3437/3492	6.9
Cleo	4600	4	8	RB	2	0.2	3443	1.3
Clinton*	4950	1	12	RB	NS	0.1	3427/3433	4.1
Davis	4575	3	4	BT	3	0.2	3443	2.7
Duffy	4793	31	30	BT,RB	29	–	3427	3.5
Grenet	5180	4	15	RB	3	1.2	3427/3422	5.8
Green Peak	5580	6	12	BT	3	2.1	3443	3.6
Jorn	5080	35	35	BT	16	–	3427/3422	6.5
Latigo	4600	2	4	–	1	0.2	3427	2.1
Little Cincha	4560	1	14	BT	2	0.1	3427	2.0
Little Duffy	4825	2	9	BT	1	0.1	3427/3491	4.0

Lula	5150	4	18	CT	2	1.2	3443	2.7
Maude	4900	4	9	BT	2	1.0	3443	2.5
Mowich	5077	54	45	BT,RB	19	–	3427/3422	4.5
North Dixie	5300	3	8	BT	5	–	3427/3491/3494	5.1
Pineridge	4526	5	19	RB	BSA Camp	–	Rd 2261	–
Pinet	4350	4	10	BT	6	0.5	3443	1.0
Ralph's	4900	2	11	BT	3	0.2	3427/3433	3.3
Raven*	5000	1	3	–	NS	0.4	3427/3491	3.5
Red Butte	5180	6	22	BT	5	0.1	3427/3422	6.1
Santiam	5125	16	40	BT	14	–	3427/3491	5.8
South Dixie	5300	2	4	BT	5	–	3427/3491/3494	4.9
Stuart*	4920	1	11	BT	NS	0.2	3427/3433	3.5
Temple	4415	11	9	RB	7	0.2	3443	2.1
Teto	4660	11	45	BT	3	0.6	3436/3437/3492	7.1
Tom's	4970	2	9	BT	1	0.4	3427	3.4
Turpentine	4690	8	29	BT	3	0.6	3443	1.1

NS = Not Surveyed XC = Cross Country CT = Cutthroat Trout
BT = Eastern Brook Trout RB = Rainbow Trout

* indicates that the lake name does not appear on most maps
Distances to lakes are the shortest distance by the easiest route.
Access trails are listed in the order of travel to the lake.

Area Discussions

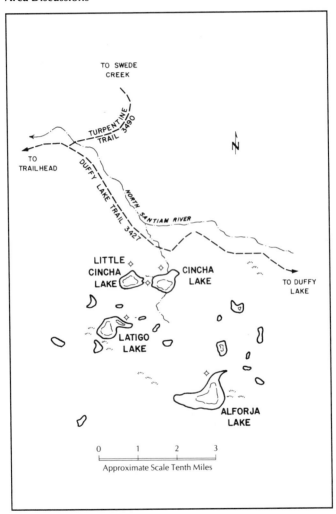

Cincha and Alforja Lakes Area Campsite Map

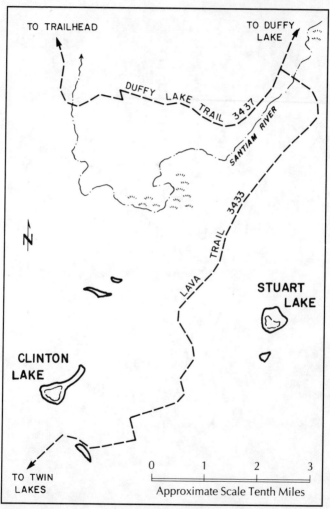

TO TRAILHEAD

TO DUFFY LAKE

DUFFY LAKE TRAIL 3437

SANTIAM RIVER

LAVA TRAIL 3433

N

STUART LAKE

CLINTON LAKE

TO TWIN LAKES

0   1   2   3

Approximate Scale Tenth Miles

Clinton and Stuart Lakes Map

Area Discussions

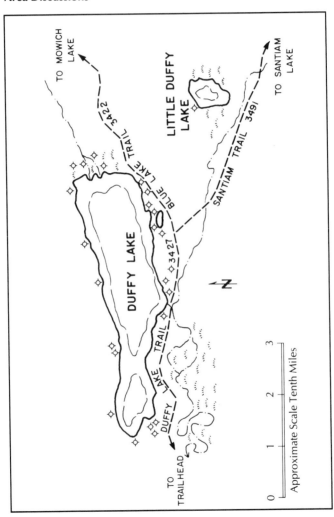

Duffy Lake Campsite Map

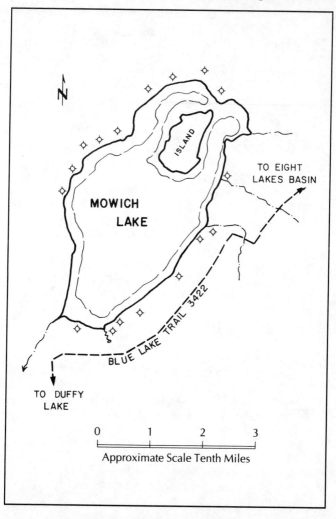

Mowich Lake Campsite Map

Area Discussions

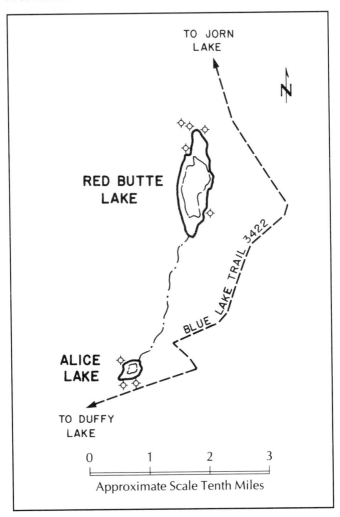

Alice and Red Butte Lakes Campsite Map

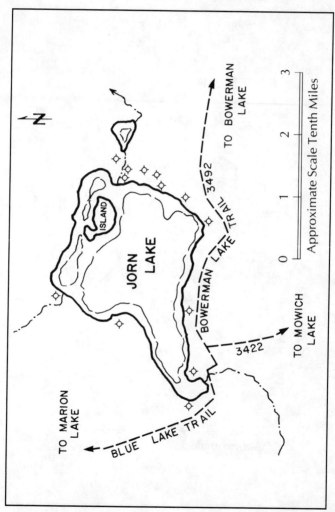

Jorn Lake Campsite Map

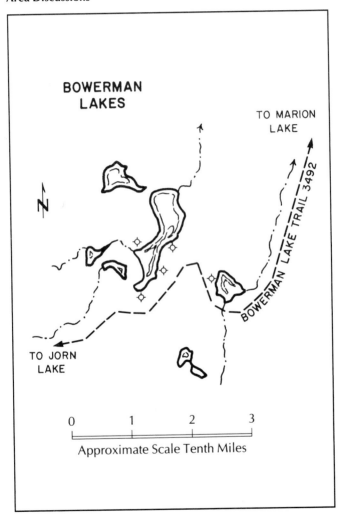

Bowerman Lakes Campsite Map

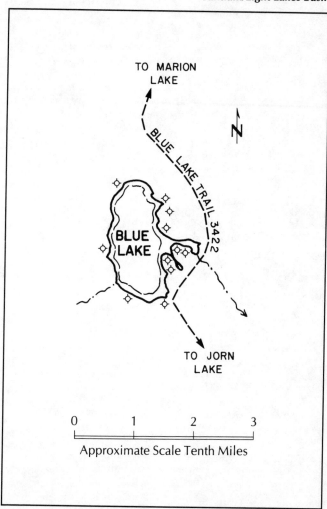

TO MARION
LAKE

N

BLUE LAKE TRAIL 3422

BLUE
LAKE

TO JORN
LAKE

0   1   2   3
Approximate Scale Tenth Miles

Area Discussions

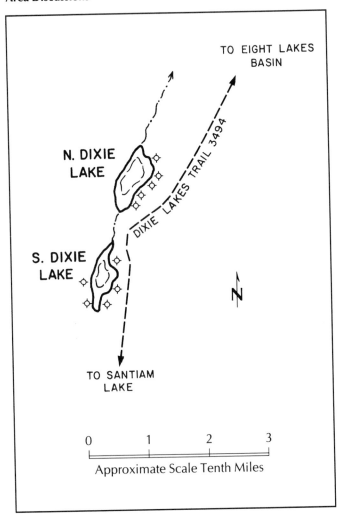

North and South Dixie Lakes Campsite Map

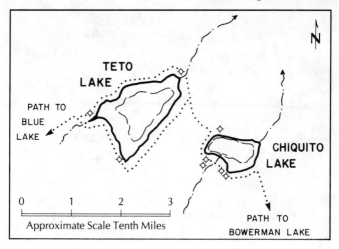

Teto and Chiquito Lakes Campsite Map

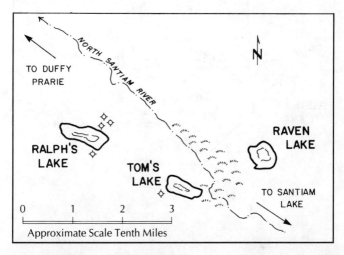

Ralph and Tom's Lakes Campsite Map

117

Area Discussions

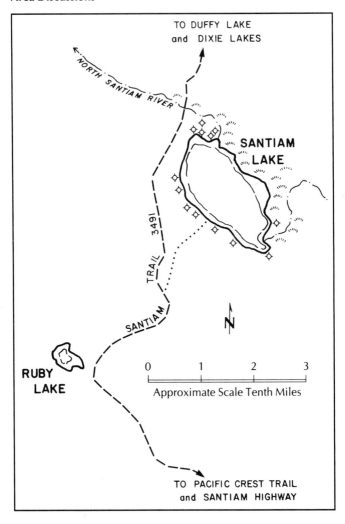

Santiam Lake Campsite Map

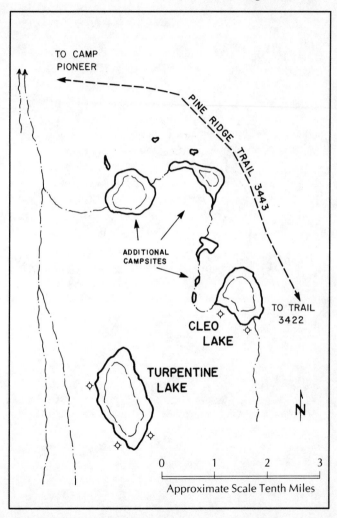

TO CAMP
PIONEER

PINE RIDGE TRAIL 3443

ADDITIONAL
CAMPSITES

TO TRAIL
3422

CLEO
LAKE

TURPENTINE
LAKE

N

| 0 | 1 | 2 | 3 |

Approximate Scale Tenth Miles

Turpentine Lake Campsite Map

119

Area Discussions

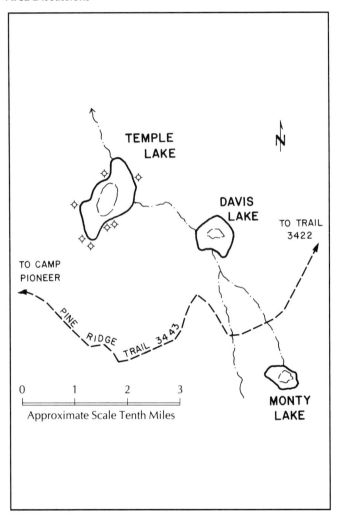

Davis, Monty and Temple Lakes Campsite Map

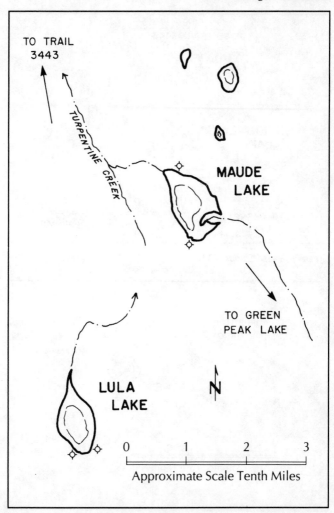

TO TRAIL
3443

TURPENTINE CREEK

MAUDE
LAKE

TO GREEN
PEAK LAKE

LULA
LAKE

N

| 0 | 1 | 2 | 3 |

Approximate Scale Tenth Miles

Lula and Maude Lakes Campsite Map

Area Discussions

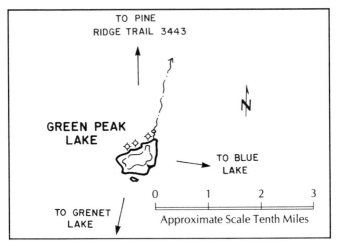

Green Peak Lake Campsite Map

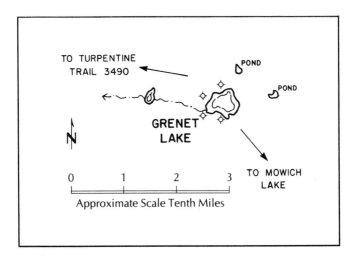

Grenet Lake Campsite Map

Maxwell Butte Area

Area Discussions

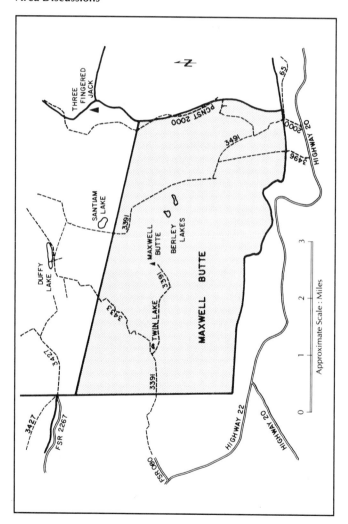

Maxwell Butte Area

MAXWELL BUTTE

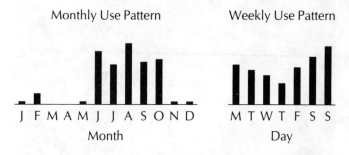

Monthly Use Pattern

J F M A M J J A S O N D
Month

Weekly Use Pattern

M T W T F S S
Day

Maxwell Butte is the most prominent feature of this area, which is located in the southwestern end of the wilderness. Because of the proximity to the Santiam Highway, you would think that it would be very popular, but in fact it receives only 2 percent of all wilderness use.

There are three entry points into the area. The most popular is the Santiam Trail 3491, which is reached via the Pacific Crest Trail 2000 access at the Santiam Highway. Almost 10 percent of all the visitors who enter the wilderness, do so by this route, although many are headed north along the Pacific Crest Trail, and east toward Square Lake. The Santiam Lodge Trail 3496, the second access, can also be used to reach the Santiam Lake Trail 3491. The Forest Service wilderness map shows this trail as an unmarked black dashed trail. The trail head is at the Santiam Lodge parking lot. Hence its name. Currently, this trail is little used. The third access is the Maxwell Butte Trail 3391. Less than 2 percent of all the wilderness visitors (only 20 to 30 people on a busy weekend) will use it to enter the area.

Area Discussions

Be sure and check the signboard at the trailhead for current rules and regulations

While there are not many lakes in the Maxwell Butte area, there still are many opportunities for dispersed camping and cross-country hiking. Use is fairly evenly distributed throughout a five-month recreation season, June to October. In the fall, this area is heavily used by deer hunters during the High Cascades season. It is also used quite a bit by skiers and winter campers.

The Berley Lakes area is the most popular destination in the Maxwell Butte area. July and August are the most popular months here. Slightly less than one-half the use occurs in August. There used to be a primitive shelter at the edge of a small meadow along the Santiam Lake Trail, approximately one mile south of the Berley Lakes. Jack Shelter, as it was called, was accidently burnt down and now is a small pile of blackened logs. I remember many a winter ski trip to this shelter, when it was entirely covered with snow. Once in-

Twin Lakes

Upper Lost Lake Creek near Berley Lakes

side, it was like a snow cave. Too bad it is gone.

The hike up Maxwell Butte is very worthwhile. From the top, you can see all the Cascade peaks along with many of the lakes in the Santiam Basin area. Duffy and Mowich Lakes are particularly noticeable. The name Mowich comes from an Indian word meaning "deer." You will be able to see some of these beautiful creatures too, if you are lucky.

Mount Jefferson Wilderness Trails
Maxwell Butte Area

Trail Name	Trail Number	Trail Dist. (Miles)	Elev. Gain (Feet)	Elev. Loss (Feet)	High Point (Feet)	Low Point (Feet)	Avg. Grade (%)	Max. Grade (%)	Access Trail Number
Maxwell Butte	3391	4.7	2759	0	6229	3470	11	13	3391
Lava	3433	2.9	380	320	5140	4780	5	18	3427
Santiam	3491	4.4	485	505	5420	5050	4	18	2000
Santiam Lodge	3496	1.8	432	30	5160	4748	5	17	3496
Pacific Crest	2000								—
Santiam Hwy to Porkupine Rdg		6.9	1670	70	6480	4880	5	14	2000/65

Mount Jefferson Wilderness Lakes
Maxwell Butte Area

Area Discussions

Lake Name	Elev. (Feet)	Size (Acres)	Depth (Feet)	Fish Species	Number of Camp Sites	XC Miles From Trail	Access Trail Number	Miles From Trail Head
Craig	5280	5	14	BT	8	0.8	3496/3491	3.7
Lower Berley	5300	6	23	CT	7	0.1	3496/3491	3.2
Maxwell	5500	1	13	CT	1	0.2	3391	3.2
Toni	4750	1	8	BT	NS	0.3	3391/3433	2.9
Train	4930	1	10	BT	4	—	3391/3433	2.6
Twin Lakes	4850	2	6	—	4	—	3391	2.2
Upper Berley	5350	6	20	BT	6	0.3	3496/3491	3.5

NS = Not Surveyed   XC = Cross Country
BT = Eastern Brook Trout   RB = Rainbow Trout   CT = Cutthroat Trout

Distances to lakes are the shortest distance by the easiest route.
Access trails are listed in the order of travel to the lake.

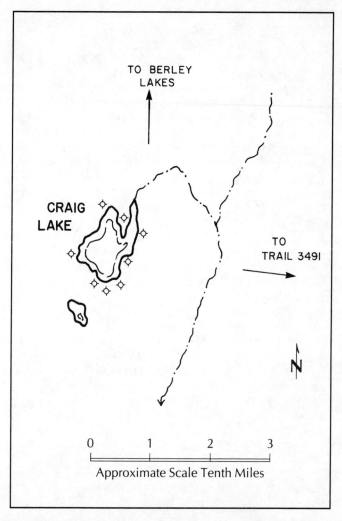

TO BERLEY
LAKES

CRAIG
LAKE

TO
TRAIL 3491

N

0   1   2   3
Approximate Scale Tenth Miles

Area Discussions

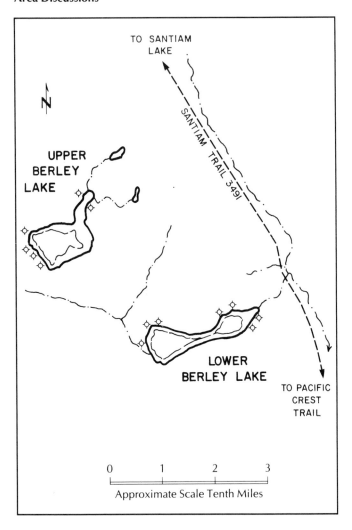

Upper and Lower Berley Lakes Campsite Map

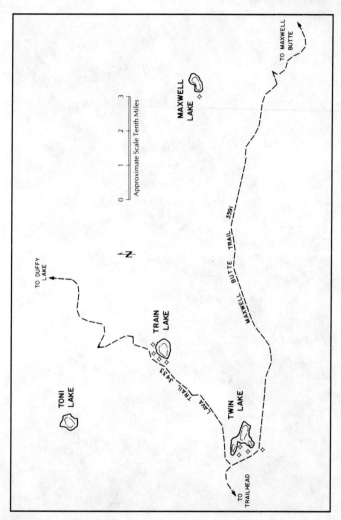

Maxwell Lake

Maxwell Butte Trail 3391

To Maxwell Butte

To Duffy Lake

Train Lake

Lava Trail 3433

Toni Lake

Twin Lake

To Trailhead

Approximate Scale Tenth Miles

0   1   2   3

N

Maxwell, Twin and Train Lakes Campsite Map

133

Three Fingered Jack is known for its many rock climbing routes

Southeast Three Fingered Jack Area

Area Discussions

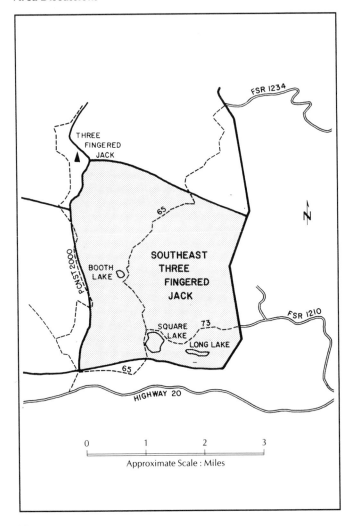

136   *Southeast Three Fingered Jack Area*

SOUTHEAST THREE FINGERED JACK

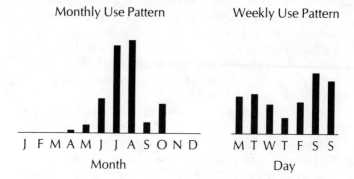

Monthly Use Pattern   Weekly Use Pattern

J F M A M J J A S O N D   M T W T F S S
Month   Day

The entire Southeast Three Fingered Jack area receives less total use than does Duffy Lake or the Hunt's Cove on the west side of the Cascades — 4 percent of the total wilderness use. While the area is no less beautiful and the weather is almost always warmer and drier, Willamette Valley residents will confront the crowds of people on the west slope, rather than drive an extra half hour to the east slope.

Access to the area is provided at three entry points. The most popular is the Pacific Crest Trail at Santiam Pass, where almost 10 percent of all trips into the wilderness are started. Since many of these trips are destined up the Pacific Crest Trail, and some into the Maxwell Butte area, only a small portion are actually headed southeast of Three Fingered Jack. Less than 2 percent of the wilderness users enter at either of the other two access points, the Round Lake Trail and the Summit Trail at Jack Lake.

Square, Long, Booth, Summit, and Martin Lakes are the most popular destinations in the area. Square Lake receives

137

about half the use in the area, while the other four lakes each receive about one-tenth of the use in the area. Obviously, if you avoid these popular sites, you will see few if any people. Almost without exception, you can camp anywhere you want, provided you have water. There are many open areas and meadows suitable for camping, and it is always a treat to make camp on pine needles and listen to the wind whistle through the pines.

When hiking the Summit Trail 65, camp can be made at First Creek, or about 0.2 miles farther north, at the two small meadows about 0.2 miles east of the trail. The old Little Lake Trail leads to these lakes, but it is no longer maintained.

Informal trails lead from the Summit Trail 65 to both Martin Lake and Summit Lake. Look for faint tracks leading west approximately 1/4 and 1/2 mile past Booth Lake. Both of these lakes are used as base camps for climbing groups. About one-half of all use at these two lakes occurs in July.

The Summit Trail used to have a trailhead at the Santiam Highway 1/2 mile south of Square Lake. Unfortunately, the parking area was inadequate and the highway turnout was unsafe. This trailhead has now been closed and the old trail abandoned. The new trail to Square Lake takes off from the Pacific Crest Trail and is quite enjoyable in its own right. The Forest Service intends to make sure that the old trail is not used, since they will ticket anyone found in the area who has entered by the old route without a wilderness permit.

Mount Jefferson Wilderness Trails
Southeast Three Finger Jack Area

Trail Name	Trail Number	Trail Dist. (Miles)	Elev. Gain (Feet)	Elev. Loss (Feet)	High Point (Feet)	Low Point (Feet)	Avg. Grade (%)	Max. Grade (%)	Access Trail Number
Summit	65								
PCT-Jack Lk		7.5	800	640	5400	4780	4	11	2000
Round Lake	73	1.9	470	0	4790	4320	5	17	73
Pacific Crest	2000								—
Santiam Hwy to Porkupine Rdg		6.9	1670	70	6480	4880	5	14	2000/65

Area Discussions

Mount Jefferson Wilderness Lakes
Southeast Three Fingered Jack Area

Lake Name	Elev. (Feet)	Size (Acres)	Depth (Feet)	Fish Species	Number of Camp Sites	XC Miles From Trail	Access Trail Number	Miles From Trail Head
Booth	5100	8	30	BT,RB	12	–	65	3.7
Long	4580	18	20	BT,RB	4	0.2	73	1.4
Martin	5380	4	18	BT,RB	7	0.7	73/65	4.2
Square	4750	55	36	BT,RB	15	–	73	1.9
Summit	5780	4	18	BT,RB	5	0.8	73/65	4.8

NS = Not Surveyed   XC = Cross Country   CT = Cutthroat Trout
BT = Eastern Brook Trout   RB = Rainbow Trout

*indicates that the lake name does not appear on most maps
Distances to lakes are the shortest distance by the easiest route.
Access trails are listed in the order of travel to the lake.

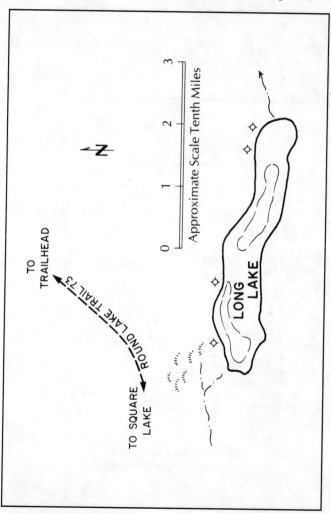

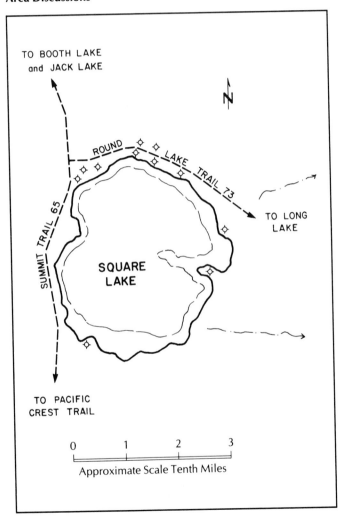

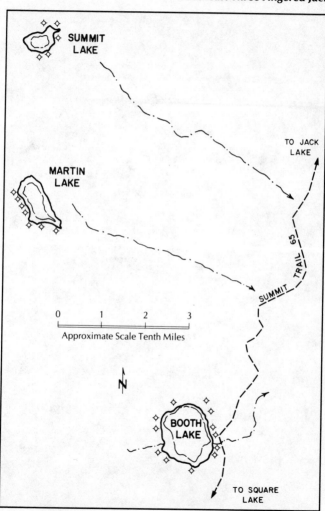

SUMMIT
LAKE

MARTIN
LAKE

TO JACK
LAKE

SUMMIT TRAIL 65

0   1   2   3
Approximate Scale Tenth Miles

N

BOOTH
LAKE

TO SQUARE
LAKE

Area Discussions

Some poorly maintained trails can be steep, eroded, and dusty

Northeast Three Fingered Jack Area

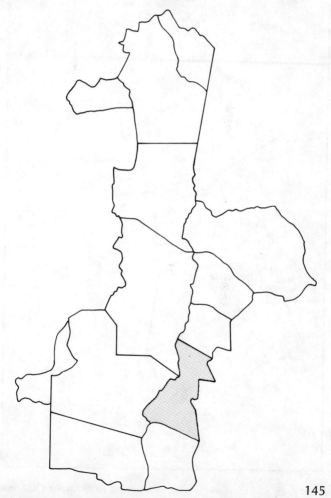

Area Discussions

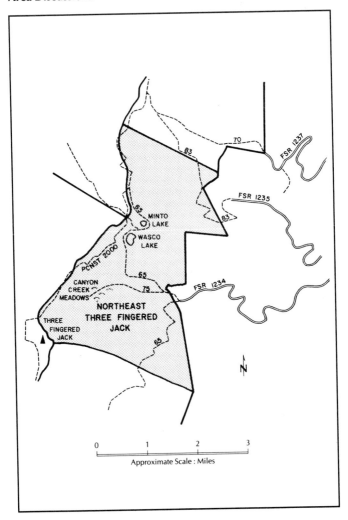

Map labels:
70
FSR 1237
83
FSR 1235
55
MINTO LAKE
83
WASCO LAKE
PCNST 2000
65
CANYON CREEK MEADOWS
75
FSR 1234
THREE FINGERED JACK
NORTHEAST THREE FINGERED JACK
65
N

```
0        1        2        3
Approximate Scale : Miles
```

NORTHEAST THREE FINGERED JACK

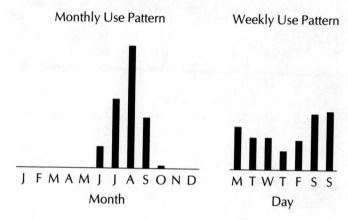

Monthly Use Pattern

J F M A M J J A S O N D
Month

Weekly Use Pattern

M T W T F S S
Day

Northeast Three Fingered Jack is the most heavily used east side area, with 6 percent of the total annual use in the Mount Jefferson Wilderness. It is accessed by two entry points, the Summit Trail 65 at Jack Lake, and the Bear Valley Trail 83. The Summit Trail is by far the most popular (7 percent of all wilderness visitors enter by this route). The Bear Valley Trail has been recently constructed and is as yet little known.

Wasco Lake is as popular as any other destination in the Northeast Three Fingered Jack area. One-half of all the use occurs in August, and on a busy weekend, 70 or more people will camp at the lake.

The name Wasco comes from the Chinook Indians. It was both the name of a tribe, and the Indian word for "basin." Perhaps the lake received its name because it sits in a small basin below the Pacific Crest Trail.

Area Discussions

One-tenth of all the use in the Northeast Three Fingered Jack area occurs at the Catlin Lakes, a group of several small lakes located west of Wasco Lake. These lakes are popular with people hiking the Pacific Crest Trail. Half of all use at these lakes occurs in July. As you hike the Pacific Crest Trail north of the lakes, watch for a viewpoint along the trail, just above Wasco Lake.

Canyon Creek Meadows is the second most popular destination in the Northeast Three Fingered Jack area. The meadows are known for good flower displays in the summer, attracting more than 70 percent of the people who visit the meadows during the month of July. There are several good places to camp, but the area does become crowded. You would be well advised to avoid the peak periods or camp higher in the valley if you desire solitude. More than 50 people will visit the meadows on a busy day.

The Canyon Creek Trail 75 is shown in the wrong location on the Forest Service wilderness map. As it currently exists, the trail proceeds farther south and uphill. It ascends past a small pond and proceeds upward, cresting the top of the ridge at an elevation of 5680 feet. From here, it switchbacks directly down to Canyon Creek. Future plans call for relocating the trail farther west, so that it does not cross the ridge at all. Instead, it will intersect the Summit Trail 65 nearer Canyon Creek, and then ascend the valley to the meadows.

A primitive trail continues past Canyon Creek Meadows, all the way up the canyon to a saddle on the south ridge of Three Fingered Jack. Here there are good views of the Cascades and the east side of Three Fingered Jack. The grade of this path is quite steep below the viewpoint. Where did Three Fingered Jack get its name? The most obvious answer is that it was named for the three pinnacles on the summit. But there is also a story that a three-fingered trapper named Jack lived in the area, and that the mountain was named after him.

The first recorded ascent of Three Fingered Jack occurred in 1923, when it was climbed by six men from Bend. Today, it is a routine climb, as Oregon mountains go, with most climbers following the south ridge route. Near the summit, the route passes east of the summit pinnacles, and the climbers can be viewed with binoculars from anywhere on the east side of the mountain.

The new Bear Valley Trail 83 has been constructed north of Jack Lake. The trail starts at a trailhead at the end of Forest Service road 1235, ascends to a small lake (I will call this

Canyon Creek Falls

Bear Valley Lake, not to be confused with Bear Lake in the South Breitenbush area). Past the lake, it follows the old Summit Trail (shown as a black dashed line on the Forest Service wilderness map) all the way to Rockpile Lake. Along the way, the trail also passes three small ponds known as the "Windy Lakes", which are unnamed on the Forest Service wilderness map. Several good camps can be made here. Since the new portion of this trail is not shown on the Forest Service wilderness map, campsite map has been provided to bridge this gap. The new trail location shown here is not exact, however, and care should be exercised when hiking the trail. Several camps can also be made in the flat portion of the upper valley near Bear Valley Lake.

From a junction with the Bear Valley Trail, the old Summit Trail also heads south and west up a ridge toward Minto Lake. It is quite distinct and easy to follow to the top of the ridge. After that, it descends and becomes obscure. From the point where the trail crosses the top of the ridge, cross-country travel to Minto Lake is not too difficult. The Forest Service may construct a new trail to Minto Lake along this route in the future. When hiking in any new area and particularly cross-country, be careful not to lose your way. This entire area has abundant wildlife, including bear, elk and deer.

Mount Jefferson Wilderness Trails
Northeast Three Fingered Jack Area

Trail Name	Trail Number	Trail Dist. (Miles)	Elev. Gain (Feet)	Elev. Loss (Feet)	High Point (Feet)	Low Point (Feet)	Avg. Grade (%)	Max. Grade (%)	Access Trail Number
Summit	65								
Jack Lk-PCT		3.5	575	265	5430	5120	5	14	65
Canyon Creek	75	2.0	760	230	5760	5230	9	13	65
Bear Valley	83	4.0	2090	0	6250	4160	10	23	83
Pacific Crest	2000								–
Porkupine Rdg to Cathedral R.		13.0	1460	2040	6480	5300	5	12	65/3437

Area Discussions

Mount Jefferson Wilderness Lakes
Northeast Three Fingered Jack Area

Lake Name	Elev. (Feet)	Size (Acres)	Depth (Feet)	Fish Species	Number of Camp Sites	XC Miles From Trail	Access Trail Number	Miles From Trail Head
Bear Valley*	4550	2	8	–	1	–	83	1.0
Catlin (Cullin)	5300	2	8	BT	NS	0.5	65/2000	3.9
Jack	5140	4	8	RB,CT	2	–	65	0.1
Koko*	5420	3	10	BT,RB, CT	2	–	65/2000	3.4
Minto	5260	6	10	CT	3	0.1	65	2.9
Wasco	5120	20	21	BT,RB	11	–	65	2.2

NS = Not Surveyed   XC = Cross Country
BT = Eastern Brook Trout   RB = Rainbow Trout   CT = Cutthroat Trout

* indicates that the lake name does not appear on most maps
Distances to lakes are the shortest distance by the easiest route.
Access trails are listed in the order of travel to the lake.

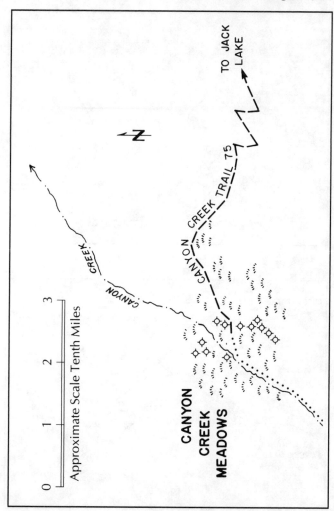

Canyon Creek Meadows Campsite Map

Area Discussions

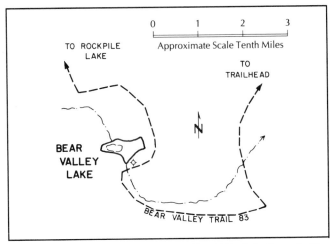

Bear Valley Lake Campsite Map

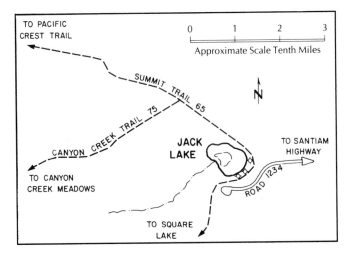

Jack Lake Trailhead and Campsite Map

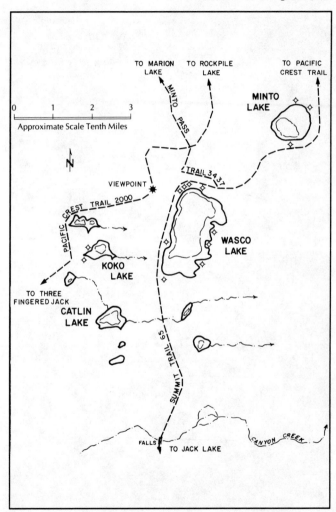

Minto, Wasco and Catlin Lakes Campsite Map

The views from the Brush Creek Trail are as fine as any in the Wilderness

Bush Creek Area

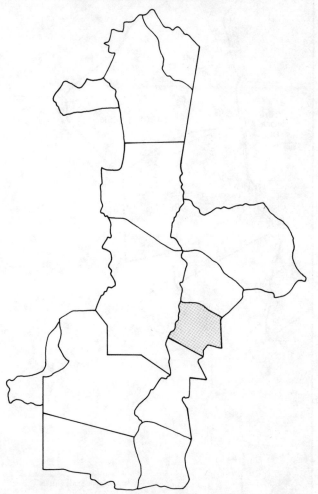

Area Discussions

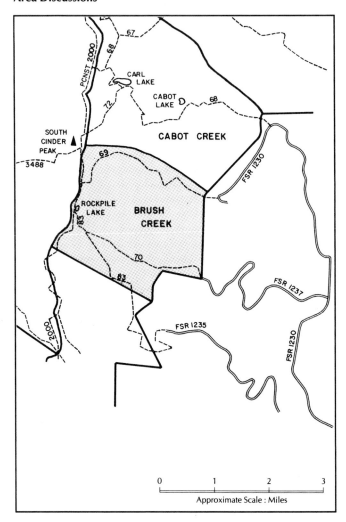

Brush Creek Area

BRUSH CREEK

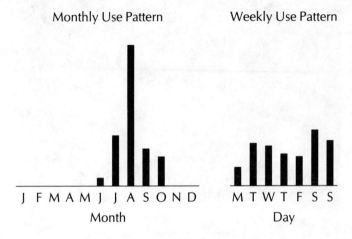

At last, we have reached the least used and least known area in the entire wilderness. The Brush Creek area had only 500 visitors in 1981, just a busy weekend worth of people at Marion Lake.

Two trails lead into the area, but neither receives much use. The Two Springs Trail 70 is reached via a rather rough and steep road. The trail intersects the Bear Valley Trail about a half mile from the Pacific Crest Trail and Rockpile Lake. The Forest Service plans to connect this trail to the lower Bear Valley Trail so that loop hikes can be made.

The Brush Creek Trail 69 is the other entry point. It can be used to complete a 10 mile loop hike to Carl Lake via the Pacific Crest Trail, the Shirley Lake Trail 72, and the Cabot Lake Trail 68. Once the loop is completed, it is an easy car shuttle from one trailhead to another, or an easy one-mile

Signs along the Brush Creek Trail

hike. There are several good places to camp along the trail, near the top of the ridge approximately 1.5 miles from the trailhead. From here, there are excellent views to the north and south—as beautiful as any in the entire wilderness. Water can be obtained from a small unnamed lake until late in the season. Several camps can be made along the Pacific Crest Trail in this area, but you will have to pack your own water late in the season.

About one mile before reaching the Pacific Crest Trail, the Brush Creek Trail descends from the crest of the ridge. At this point, it is extremely narrow, with steep side slopes and many sharp switchbacks. It is not recommended for live-stock. From the junction with the old Summit Trail (black dashed line on Forest Service wilderness map), the trail has

North Cinder Peak

been routed south towards Rockpile Lake, where it intersects the Pacific Crest Trail on the ridge, 0.4 miles north of the lake. As seen from the Pacific Crest Trail, the junction is marked by a wood post. The trail has been relocated in an effort to avoid the old route across a broad cinder field (red dashed line on map), where the tread is indistinct and erosion a serious potential problem.

Rockpile Lake is the most popular and heavily used destination in the area. It is the only lake along the Pacific Crest Trail between Santiam Pass and Shale Lake. Consequently, it is a regularly used camping spot. If all you want to do is hike for a weekend, I recommend you leave Rockpile Lake for those who are hiking the Pacific Crest Trail.

Mount Jefferson Wilderness Trails
Brush Creek Area

Trail Name	Trail Number	Trail Dist. (Miles)	Elev. Gain (Feet)	Elev. Loss (Feet)	High Point (Feet)	Low Point (Feet)	Avg. Grade (%)	Max. Grade (%)	Access Trail Number
Brush Creek	69	3.2	1410	360	6420	5100	10	27	69
Two Springs	70	2.4	890	0	5760	4870	7	13	70
Bear Valley	83	4.0	2090	0	6250	4160	10	23	83
Pacific Crest	2000								—
Porkupine Rdg to Cathedral R.		13.0	1460	2040	6480	5300	5	12	65/3437

Mount Jefferson Wilderness Lakes
Brush Creek Area

Lake Name	Elev. (Feet)	Size (Acres)	Depth (Feet)	Fish Species	Number of Camp Sites	XC Miles From Trail	Access Trail Number	Miles From Trail Head
Rockpile	6240	NS	NS	–	10	–	83	3.1

NS = Not Surveyed
BT = Eastern Brook Trout

XC = Cross Country
RB = Rainbow Trout

CT = Cutthroat Trout

Distances to lakes are the shortest distance by the easiest route.
Access trails are listed in the order of travel to the lake.

Area Discussions

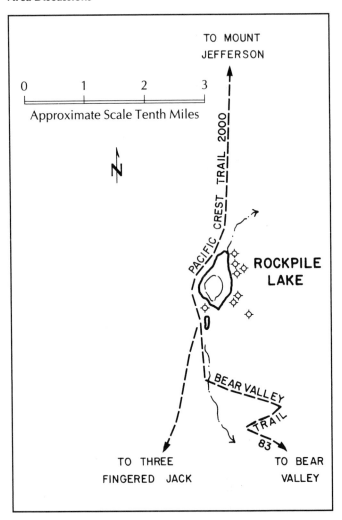

TO MOUNT
JEFFERSON

0   1   2   3
Approximate Scale Tenth Miles

N

PACIFIC CREST TRAIL 2000

ROCKPILE
LAKE

BEAR VALLEY

TRAIL
83

TO THREE
FINGERED JACK

TO BEAR
VALLEY

Rockpile Lake Campsite Map

Cabot Creek Area

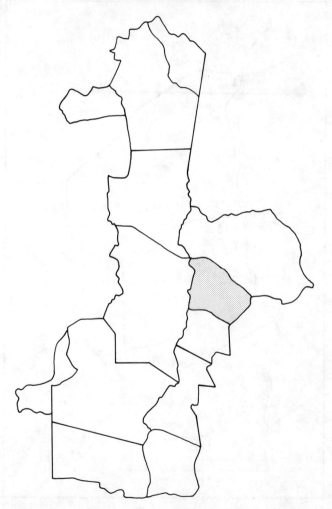

Area Discussions

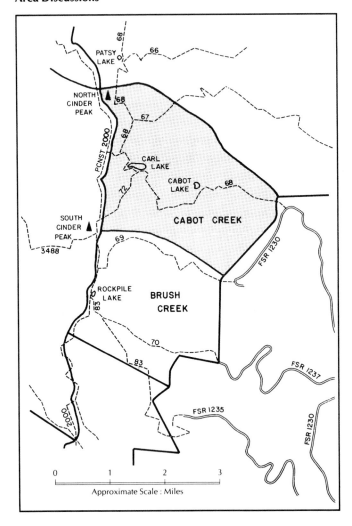

Cabot Creek Area

CABOT CREEK

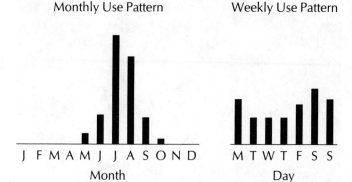

Monthly Use Pattern   Weekly Use Pattern

J F M A M J J A S O N D   M T W T F S S

Month   Day

This is the second most heavily used area on the east side of the Cascade crest, with a total of 4 percent of all the use in the Mount Jefferson Wilderness. The only access is the Cabot Lake Trail 68. A trail which stretches all the way to Hole-in-the-Wall Park. On a busy weekend, well over 100 people may be found using this trail.

Cabot and Carl Lakes are equally popular destinations. Each lake receives more than 45 percent of all the use in the Cabot Creek area. Both Lakes have limited opportunities for alternate nearby camping due to topographic constraints. As a result, if you are planning a trip in this area during the peak season, you may want to consider an alternate destination such as any of the three ponds before Carl Lake. With less than 10 percent of all use occurring in the remainder of the area, there are many opportunities for solitude.

A new trail segment, the Shirley Lake Trail 72, has been constructed from Carl Lake to the Pacific Crest Trail north of

Carl Lake

South Cinder Peak. As mentioned in the Brush Creek Section, this trail can be used to complete a loop hike using the Cabot Lake Trail 68 and the Brush Creek Trail 69.

Campsites are available along the Cabot Lake Trail between Carl Lake and Patsy Lake. Several camps can be made near small ponds and open areas along the trail above Carl Lake, about 0.6 miles before Junction Lake. A few camps can be located at Junction Lake, though this is only a small pond, and could become quite crowded. Beyond Junction Lake, there are several more open areas where good camps could be made, including near the top of the broad pass before reaching Patsy Lake. Water may have to be carried to these latter sites.

The terrain around Forked Butte is quite interesting. Just before reaching the Forked Butte lava flow, there are some outstanding examples of glacial rock polish on both sides of the trail. These are places which at one time were under at least 100 feet of ice. Over the years, they were slowly ground smooth by ice and rock. Later, the glaciers retreated to reveal the smooth rocks which we see today. Look for rounded humps of rock with longitudinal groves scratched in the surface. Farther up the trail, just before reaching the pass near North Cinder Peak, the Forked Butte lava flow is adjacent to a talus (rock debris) slope. Here you can see how the light-colored talus has fallen on the older and darker lava.

Carl Lake is actually a large glacial tarn which was scooped out of solid rock by ancient glaciers. If you climb the ridge to the north, you will see how the lake is enclosed by only the thinnest of rock ridges on the north side. Perhaps someday it will breach this rock enclosure and become a high mountain meadow.

Glacial rock polish and striations on rocks near Forked Butte Lava Flow

Area Discussions

Do stay up long enough some night to look at the stars—here Mount Jefferson is silhouetted by the aurora borealis

Mount Jefferson Wilderness Trails
Cabot Creek Area

Trail Name	Trail Number	Trail Dist. (Miles)	Elev. Gain (Feet)	Elev. Loss (Feet)	High Point (Feet)	Low Point (Feet)	Avg. Grade (%)	Max. Grade (%)	Access Trail Number
Cabot Lake	68								68
Trhead to Carl Lk		5.1	970	0	5540	4570	4	11	–
Carl Lk to Patsy Lk		3.7	600	870	6030	5270	8	17	68/67
Shirley Lake	72	1.5	740	0	6280	5540	9	15	68
Pacific Crest	2000								–
Porkupine Rdg to Cathedral R.		13.0	1460	2040	6480	5300	5	12	65/3437

Area Discussions

Mount Jefferson Wilderness Lakes
Cabot Creek Area

Lake Name	Elev. (Feet)	Size (Acres)	Depth (Feet)	Fish Species	Number of Camp Sites	XC Miles From Trail	Access Trail Number	Miles From Trail Head
Cabot	4660	6	18	BT,RB	12	0.1	68	1.9
Carl	5490	20	51	BT,RB	13	—	68	4.8
First Pond*	5280	1	NS	—	3	—	68	3.7
Junction Lake	5900	NS	NS	—	3	—	67/68	7.6
Second Pond*	5280	1	NS	—	1	—	68	3.9
Shirley	5580	4	11	BT,RB	6	0.1	68/72	5.3
Third Pond*	5360	2	NS	—	4	—	68	4.3

NS = Not Surveyed   XC = Cross Country   CT = Cutthroat Trout
BT = Eastern Brook Trout   RB = Rainbow Trout

Distances to lakes are the shortest distance by the easiest route.
Access trails are listed in the order of travel to the lake.

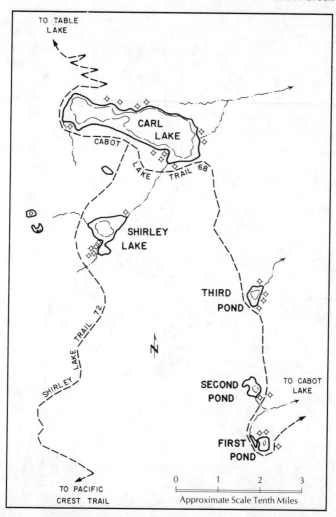

Carl and Shirley Lakes Campsite Map

Area Discussions

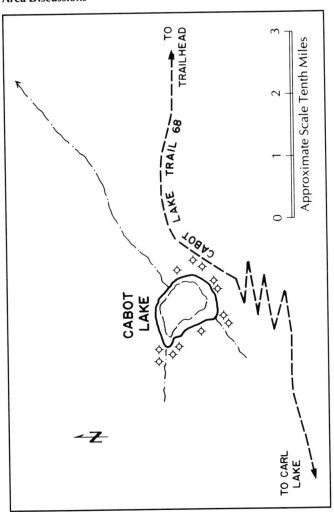

Cabot Lake Campsite Map

Jefferson Creek Area

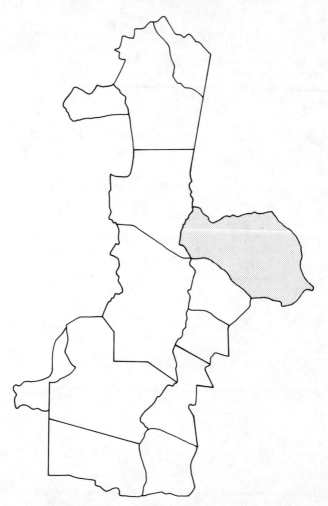

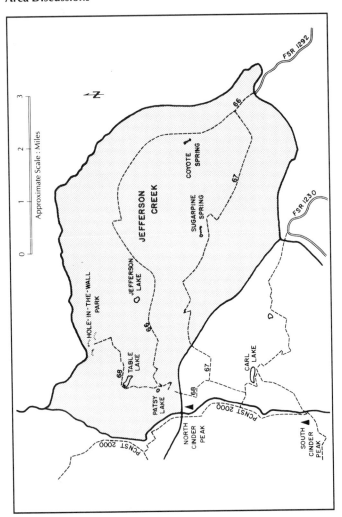

Jefferson Creek Area

JEFFERSON CREEK

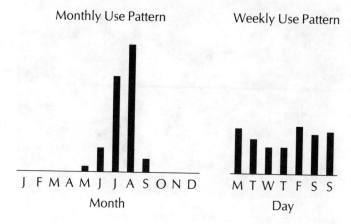

Monthly Use Pattern

Weekly Use Pattern

J F M A M J J A S O N D
Month

M T W T F S S
Day

Larger than any other area in the Mount Jefferson Wilderness, the Jefferson Creek area receives 1 percent of the total wilderness use. Only the Brush Creek area, which is 1/3 the size, receives less use.

There is only one entry point into the area, the Jefferson Lake Trail 66. However, only 0.7 miles from the trailhead, the trail forks to create the Sugarpine Trail 67.

Jefferson Creek is the most remote and out-of-the-way area in the wilderness. All of the major destinations are more than 6 miles from the trailhead. Table Lake and Patsy Lake are the two most popular destinations. Combined, they account for 65 percent of all the use in the Jefferson Creek area. Even so, on a typical crowded weekend you will see less than 70 people. August is the time when both lakes are the most heavily used. If you choose to avoid these two areas, you will be rewarded with virtual solitude and innumerable places to camp.

Mount Jefferson from the viewpoint above Hole-in-the-Wall Park

The Jefferson Creek lava flow is just one of the many remarkable geologic features of the area. It stretches for more than 10 miles from its source at the base of Bear Butte, almost all the way to the Metolius River. As you hike the Jefferson Lake Trail, you will follow the flow for about 6 miles. Watch to see how the plants and trees are reclaiming a sterile rocky world. Hundreds of years from now, a new forest will stand where today there are only barren rocks baking in the sun.

The Table, a flat-topped twin mesa west of Table Lake, is another interesting feature. Although it is steep on all sides, a scramble to the top delights you with views of Mount Jefferson across a flat park-like area. It offers acres of open space to camp, but you may need to bring your own water late in the season.

Hole-in-the-wall Park is over 10 miles from the nearest trail head, and few people take the time to see it. Tucked in a

178

very deep steep-sided glacially carved canyon, the "Park" is an intricate network of wet meadow, ponds and streams. There is a very good viewpoint overlooking the Park on the ridge west of Bear Point. From here, it is easy to see how Hole-in-the-Wall Park got its name. A major portion of the Park is within the Warm Springs Indian Reservation, and therefore is off limits to camping. Nevertheless, it is a nice place to visit. Count the number of switchbacks as you descend to the bottom. There are a number of alternative campsites on the way to Hole-in-the-Wall Park, along the Cabot Lake Trail.

It seems appropriate here to give a brief history of this, the second highest peak in Oregon. It was first reported seen by Lewis and Clark in March, 1806, when they observed it from a point near the mouth of the Willamette River. They named it in honor of Thomas Jefferson. The first recorded ascent of the mountain came in August 1888, when Ed Cross and Ray Farmer of Salem made it up the south ridge. The first ascent of the north route was also in August, this time in 1903. The climb was made solo—a remarkable feat considering the type of equipment that was (or was not) available at that time, and the fact that even today, the north route is still considered one of the most challenging in the state.

There are many other places in the Jefferson Creek area which are suitable for camping. The area 1 mile northwest of Patsy Lake contains many additional small lakes and meadows. Between Patsy Lake and Table Lake, off the Cabot Lake Trail, there are a number of flat open areas with close proximity to water. There is even a lake in the top of the cinder cone south of The Table, but I doubt if you would want to camp there. As in all areas of the wilderness, no-trace camp-

Area Discussions

Hole-in-the-Wall Park

ing should be the rule. Do not build new fire rings, and only burn fires if absolutely necessary.

As mentioned above, a 19-mile extended loop trip can be accomplished via the Jefferson Lake Trail 66, the Cabot Lake Trail 68, and the Sugarpine Trail 67. Several potential campsites have already been described in the Cabot Creek Section. Additional camps can be made in a broad saddle between Forked Butte and Sugarpine Ridge, and on top of Sugarpine Ridge. Water is available from nearby streams and springs on the south side of the ridge. When hiking the Sugarpine Trail 67, be aware that Sugarpine Springs is not marked at the correct location on the Forest Service wilderness map. Instead of being at 5750 feet as shown on the map, a sign points the way to the springs at an elevation of approximately 5100 feet—a welcome spot on a warm summer day.

Patsy Lake is very small, with very few (if any) "good" campsites. Because it is at a trail junction, it receives more use than it should. Therefore, you may need to consider alternate camps when in this area. If there are no other camps available, there is some flat area just down the hill from Patsy Lake along the Jefferson Lake Trail 66, where it skirts a lava flow.

If you are hiking the Pacific Crest Trail in this area, there are several potential campsites on the ridge above Patsy Lake, north of North Cinder Peak. This is a very exposed area, though, and could only be used in good weather. There is a small lake on the north side of North Cinder Peak, approximately 0.1 mile east of where the trail crosses a small cinder flat. It may be possible to camp here in more inclement weather, since it is somewhat more sheltered from south winds.

Mount Jefferson and The Table from the Pacific Crest Trail

Mount Jefferson Wilderness Trails
Jefferson Creek Area

Trail Name	Trail Number	Trail Dist. (Miles)	Elev. Gain (Feet)	Elev. Loss (Feet)	High Point (Feet)	Low Point (Feet)	Avg. Grade (%)	Max. Grade (%)	Access Trail Number
Jefferson Lake	66	8.3	2270	40	5300	3090	5	15	66
Sugar Pine	67	6.7	3195	465	5920	3190	10	21	66
Cabot Lake	68								68
Carl Lk to Patsy Lk		3.7	600	870	6030	5270	8	17	68/67
Patsy Lk to Hole-in		3.4	810	840	5860	5240	9	23	68/66
Pacific Crest	2000								—
Porkupine Rdg to Cathedral R.		13.0	1460	2040	6480	5300	5	12	65/3437

183

Mount Jefferson Wilderness Lakes
Jefferson Creek Area

Lake Name	Elev. (Feet)	Size (Acres)	Depth (Feet)	Fish Species	Number of Camp Sites	XC Miles From Trail	Access Trail Number	Miles From Trail Head
Jefferson	4750	4	6	–	2	0.3	66	6.6
Patsy	5240	2	18	BT	3	–	66	8.3
Table	5470	5	13	BT	12	–	66/68	9.3

NS = Not Surveyed   XC = Cross Country
BT = Eastern Brook Trout   RB = Rainbow Trout   CT = Cutthroat Trout

Distances to lakes are the shortest distance by the easiest route.
Access trails are listed in the order of travel to the lake.

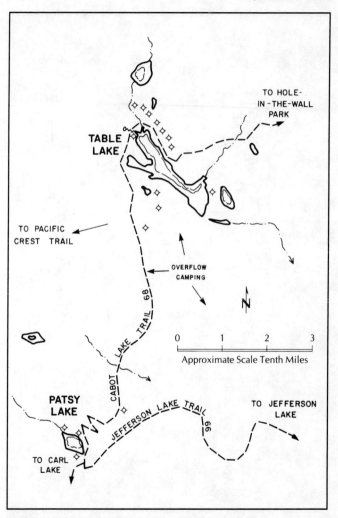

TO HOLE-
IN-THE-WALL
PARK

**TABLE
LAKE**

TO PACIFIC
CREST TRAIL

OVERFLOW
CAMPING

CABOT LAKE TRAIL 68

N

| 0 | 1 | 2 | 3 |

Approximate Scale Tenth Miles

**PATSY
LAKE**

JEFFERSON LAKE TRAIL 66

TO JEFFERSON
LAKE

TO CARL
LAKE

Table and Patsy Lakes Campsite Map

Area Discussions

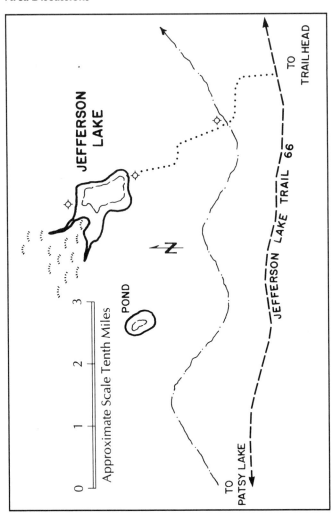

Jefferson Lake Campsite Map

Big Meadows Area

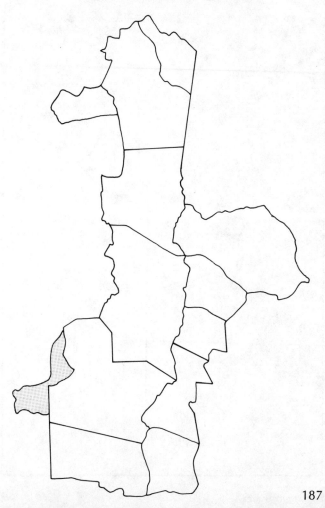

Area Discussions

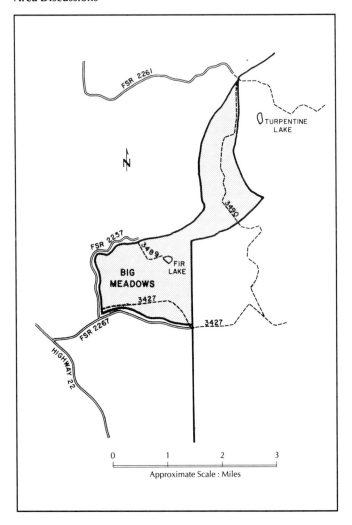

Big Meadows Area

BIG MEADOWS RECREATION AREA

The Big Meadows Recreation Area is on the west side of the Mount Jefferson Wilderness (see campsite map). There are no use statistics available for the area, since it is not in the wilderness. Past experience has demonstrated that the area is little used, relative to other more popular areas within the wilderness. Currently, the Forest Service manages the area as a dispersed recreation area, allowing some timber harvest, with an emphasis on management of the area for recreation. The area is used for hiking, fishing, horse riding, and hunting in the summer, and cross country skiing in the winter.

There are many areas both adjacent to the area and within the area suitable for camping. Because it has easy road access, it is ideal for family camping and hiking. Many users establish car camps near the meadows and take day trips into the area, both on foot and on horseback. Fay Lake also has opportunities for car camping. Future plans call for the construction of developed campsites (picnic tables, fire rings, and pit toilets) and loop trails for hiking and horse riding. An inquiry to the Detroit Ranger District will give the most current information on facilities available in the area.

Access to the area is provided by Forest Service Road 2257, which forms part of the area boundary, and by the Duffy Lake Trail 3427 and the Pika-Fir Trail 3489. The latter trail is not shown on the Mount Jefferson wilderness map, but it is marked on the more recent Detroit District "Fireman's" map. As the name implies, the trail leads to Pika and Fir Lakes. There is a good viewpoint overlooking Big Meadows about 0.2 miles south of Pika Lake. Future plans call for a Forest Service trail to this point, but now it is partially blazed and mostly cross-country.

Area Discussions

The Duffy Lake Trail 3427, which takes off from Road 2257, is an alternate route into the Mount Jefferson Wilderness. It intersects the main Duffy Lake Trail approximately 0.25 miles from the new trailhead and parking area. There are many places along the trail which would make good campsites, but there are no existing campsites. The trail is mostly flat for the first mile and very suitable for family outings.

(Author's Note: As this book goes to press, the Big Meadows area has been included in the Oregon Wilderness Bill as a proposed addition to the Mount Jefferson Wilderness. Should this area become wilderness, the present management direction will be changed and some of the information in this section will no longer be correct.)

Mount Jefferson Wilderness Trails
Big Meadows Area

Trail Name	Trail Number	Trail Dist. (Miles)	Elev. Gain (Feet)	Elev. Loss (Feet)	High Point (Feet)	Low Point (Feet)	Avg. Grade (%)	Max. Grade (%)	Access Trail Number
Duffy Lake	3427								
Big Meadows (Alt)		2.3	550	20	4090	3560	8	19	3427A
Pika-Fir	3489	0.9	210	30	4070	3880	5	14	3489

Mount Jefferson Wilderness Lakes
Big Meadows Area

Lake Name	Elev. (Feet)	Size (Acres)	Depth (Feet)	Fish Species	Number of Camp Sites	XC Miles From Trail	Access Trail Number	Miles From Trail Head
Fay	3825	6	15	BT,RB	3	–	Rd 2257	–
Fir	4025	6	20	BT	2	–	3489	0.9
Pika	3920	3	14	BT	1	–	3489	0.5
Widgeon	4320	3	13	BT	NS	0.7	3489	1.6

NS = Not Surveyed   XC = Cross Country
BT = Eastern Brook Trout   RB = Rainbow Trout   CT = Cutthroat Trout

Distances to lakes are the shortest distance by the easiest route.
Access trails are listed in the order of travel to the lake.

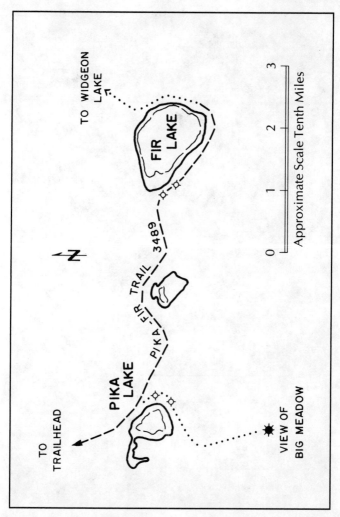

Fir and Pika Lakes Campsite Map

The Triangulation Trail is an easy and fun hike for children

Triangulation Peak Area

Area Discussions

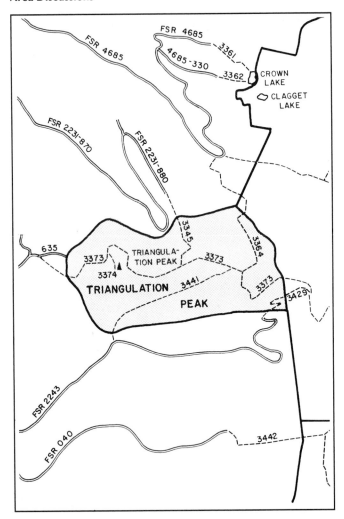

Triangulation Peak Area

TRIANGULATION PEAK RECREATION AREA

Like the Big Meadows area, the Triangulation Peak Recreation Area is not within the Mount Jefferson Wilderness, and therefore there is no information on the current amount of use. Because the area contains an extensive trail network which leads into the wilderness, it receives more hiking use than does the Big Meadows area. However, it is not as heavily used for camping, horse riding or skiing.

The Forest Service wilderness map shows all of the trails in the area, but unfortunately, the road access and trailhead to the Triangulation Trail 3373 are shown incorrectly. A Forest Service road now runs all the way to where the Triangulation Trail 3373 used to intersect the old Outerson Mountain Trail. The road now follows the old Outerson Trail. The Triangulation Trail 3373 trailhead is now at the junction of Road 2233-650 and 2233-635. There was a trail sign in 1982, but there is no information board or permit box. If you intend to enter the wilderness using this trail, you must obtain your wilderness permit at the Detroit District office on the way to the trail.

The Triangulation Trail 3373 and the Devils Ridge Trail 3345 both follow the ridge tops and therefore offer outstanding views of the Cascades and Mount Jefferson. The Cheat Creek Trail 3441 climbs a rugged valley below Triangulation Peak, taking you through an interesting meadow on the way to the Triangulation Trail on the ridge.

The Triangulation Trail is very suitable for family-oriented day hikes. The short hike to the summit of Triangulation Peak on the Triangulation Peak Trail 3374 is not too difficult for children, and the summit is a great place to eat lunch and admire the scenery.

Area Discussions

Spire Rock is a special feature that might attract the rock climber. There are many difficult pitches which would challenge even the best of climbers, as well as some easier training pitches. Ropes would be recommended for all climbs.

Boca Cave on the east side of Triangulation Peak is a large natural arched cave well worth exploring. It can be seen from the Triangulation Trail in the saddle east of Triangulation Peak. It is best reached by hiking to the secondary summit of Triangulation Peak, and then traveling east along the ridge, dropping down to reach the cave entrance.

There are few locations in the area where campsites can be made. A several people could camp on the broad secondary summit of Triangulation Peak. Camps can be made near Wild Cheat Meadow, and there is a good campsite on Devil's Ridge about 0.25 miles north of the Triangulation Trail. Camps can also be made in several open areas off the Craig Trail 3364, just north of the Triangulation Trail junction. All of these camps, except the Wild Cheat sites, are on the ridge tops, and weather conditions should be considered before establishing camps in these locations.

Future Forest Service plans for the area include geologic interpretive signs and perhaps the construction of a loop trail with the Cheat Creek Trail 3441. Consult with the Detroit Ranger District for further information on the management of the area.

(Author's Note: As this book goes to press, the Triangulation Peak area has been included in the Oregon Wilderness Bill as a proposed addition to the Mount Jefferson Wilderness. Should this area become wilderness, the present management direction will be changed and some of the information in this section will no longer be correct.)

Mount Jefferson Wilderness Trails
Triangulation Peak Area

Trail Name	Trail Number	Trail Dist. (Miles)	Elev. Gain (Feet)	Elev. Loss (Feet)	High Point (Feet)	Low Point (Feet)	Avg. Grade (%)	Max. Grade (%)	Access Trail Number
Devils Ridge	3345	1.3	480	80	4960	4480	8	12	3345
Craig	3364	2.7	1900	240	4900	3000	15	18	3364
Triangulation	3373	6.2	1020	790	5280	4660	5	16	3373
Triangulation Peak	3374	0.6	554	0	5434	4880	17	17	3373
Whitewater	3429	4.2	1360	0	5560	4200	6	13	3429
Cheat Creek	3441	2.9	1820	0	4760	2940	12	17	3441

APPENDIX A

AGENCY DIRECTORY AND ADDRESSES

Federal Agencies—USDA Forest Service

Deschutes National Forest
Forest Supervisor's Office
211 N.E. Revere Street
Bend, Oregon 97701

Deschutes National Forest
Sisters Ranger District Office
P.O. Box 249
Sisters, Oregon 97759

Mount Hood National Forest
Forest Supervisor's Office
19559 S.E. Division
Gresham, Oregon 97030

Mount Hood National Forest
Clackamas Ranger District Office
61431 East Highway 224
Estacada, Oregon 97203

Willamette National Forest
Forest Supervisor's Office
Federal Building
211 East 7th Avenue
Eugene, Oregon 97401

Willamette National Forest
Detroit Ranger District
Star Route, Box 320
Mill City, Oregon 97360

State Agencies

Oregon Department of Fish and Wildlife
State Office
506 S.W. Mill Street
P.O. Box 3503
Portland, Oregon 97208

Other Agencies

Confederated Tribes of the Warm Springs Indian Reservation
Warm Springs Indian Reservation
Warm Springs, Oregon 97761

APPENDIX B

OUTDOOR GROUP DIRECTORY AND ADDRESSES

Chemeketans, Inc.
360 1/2 State Street NE
Salem, Oregon 97301

Mazamas
909 N.W. 19th Avenue
Portland, Oregon 97209

Obsidians, Inc.
P.O. Box 322
Eugene, Oregon 97440

Sierra Club
2637 S.W. Water Street
Portland, Oregon 97201

APPENDIX C

HORSE AND LLAMA OUTFITTERS

Mr. Bill Earlywine
Blue Lake Corrals
Star Route
Sisters, Oregon 97759

High Cascade Pack Station
70775 Indian Ford Ranch Road
Sisters, Oregon 97759

Gary L. Jelinek
Oregon Wilderness Llama Tours
P.O. Box 7515
Eugene, Oregon 97401

Mr. Jim Pyeatt
Licensed Guide and Outfitter
P.O. Box 13
Lostine, Oregon 97857

Rainbow Packing (Llama)
Daniel S. Emrich
69505 Camp Polk Road
Sisters, Oregon 97759

APPENDIX D

REFERENCES

Route Finding

Land Navigation Handbook
The Sierra Club Guide to Map and Compass
W. S. Kals
Sierra Club Books, 1983

Staying Found
The Complete Map and Compass Handbook
June Fleming
Vintage Books, 1982

Backpacking

Backpacking One Step at a Time
Harvey Manning
Vintage Books, 1980

Mountaineering

Mountaineering, The Freedom of the Hills
Peggy Ferber, et al
The Mountaineers, 1974

A Climbing Guide to Oregon
Nicholas A. Dodge
The Touchstone Press, 1975

Hiking

60 Oregon Hiking Trails—Central Oregon Cascades
Don and Roberta Lowe
The Touchstone Press, 1978

The Pacific Crest Trail
Volume 2: Oregon And Washington
Jeffrey P. Schaffer, Bev and Fred Hartline
Wilderness Press, 1979

Fishing

Henning's Oregon Guide
Fishing—Hunting—Vacation
Henning Helstrom
Helstrom Publications, Inc., 1980

Mount Jefferson Wilderness
Lake Index

Mount Jefferson Wilderness
Trails Index

Notes

Notes